T0301999

Structured for Success
What Leaders Need to Know to Build and Sustain Effective Organizations

Structured for Success
What Leaders Need to Know to Build and Sustain Effective Organizations

By

J. Chris White

CRC Press
Taylor & Francis Group
Boca Raton London New York

CRC Press is an imprint of the
Taylor & Francis Group, an **informa** business

A PRODUCTIVITY PRESS BOOK

First published 2018 by Productivity Press

Published 2021 by CRC Press
Taylor & Francis Group
6000 Broken Sound Parkway NW, Suite 300
Boca Raton, FL 33487-2742

First issued in paperback 2021

ISBN 13: 978-1-03-224189-0 (pbk)
ISBN 13: 978-1-4987-6440-7 (hbk)

Library of Congress Cataloging-in-Publication Data

Names: White, J. Chris, author.
Title: Structured for success: what leaders need to know to build and sustain effective organizations / J. Chris White.
Description: Boca Raton, FL: CRC Press, 2018. | Includes index.
Identifiers: LCCN 2017048519 | ISBN 9781498764407 (hardback: alk. paper)
Subjects: LCSH: Leadership. | Organizational effectiveness.
Classification: LCC HD57.7 .W4584 2018 | DDC 658.4/092–dc23
LC record available at https://lccn.loc.gov/2017048519

Visit the Taylor & Francis Web site at
http://www.taylorandfrancis.com

and the CRC Press Web site at
http://www.crcpress.com

Contents

Overview Summary: The Entire Book in a Few Pages ix
Book Sections Descriptions...xiii
Acknowledgments xvii
About the Author xix

SECTION 1   SYSTEMS AND STRUCTURE

1   Leaders as Masters of Structure...3
  A Silly Example...4
  The Goal of This Book...5
  Moving from SNAPSHOTS to PATTERNS 8
  Moving from LINES to LOOPS 10
  Moving from ONE to MANY..11
  Why Does This Matter?..12
  Bibliography 13

2   Feedback Loops as System Structure..15
  Positive (Reinforcing) Feedback Loop...16
  Negative (Balancing) Feedback Loop 20
  Combinations of Feedback Loops and the Common S-Curve..........................23
  Combinations of Multiple Feedback Loops and Resulting Behaviors................28
  The Kaibab Plateau 35
  So Why Does This Matter?...37
  Bibliography 39

SECTION 2   CONSEQUENCE MAPS

3   Creating Consequence Maps..43
  Team-Based Development 43
  Nouns and Relationships 44
  Laundry Lists and Circles 46
  Cause-and-Effect Connections...47
  Identify Feedback Loops..48

What Happens Next? 50
Close the Loops 50
Use Lots of Space..51
Real-World Example: Asset Management for a City
Water Delivery System...51
A Final Comment..59
Bibliography 59

4   **Example Consequence Map for a City for a Major Change Initiative.....61**
The Feedback Loops 61
The Full Consequence Map 72
What Does the Consequence Map Show Us? 75
Final Remarks... 77

5   **Example Consequence Map for a Non-Profit Organization for**
Grant Proposals...79
The Full Consequence Map 80
The Feedback Loops 82
What Does the Consequence Map Show Us? 86
Final Remarks..88

6   **Example Consequence Map for a Management Culture within a**
Defense Contractor Program 91
The Full Consequence Map 92
The Feedback Loops 98
What Does the Consequence Map Show Us? 102
Final Remarks..106

SECTION 3   SYSTEM DYNAMICS SIMULATION

7   **Simulation Using System Dynamics 111**
Statistical Modeling and Structure Modeling 112
Overview of System Dynamics Modeling and Simulation Methodology....... 119
Some Final Comments on System Dynamics Modeling 124
Bibliography 125

8   **Example Simulation for Reduction in Force (RIF) 127**
The Full Consequence Map 127
The Feedback Loops 131
The Simulation Model 134
Simulation Scenarios and Results 141
Final Remarks.. 149

9   **Example Simulation for Project Management**........................**151**
  The Full Consequence Map 151
  The Feedback Loops 154
  The Simulation Model 158
  Simulation Scenarios and Results 164
  Final Remarks...171
  Bibliography 172

SECTION 4   STRUCTURED FOR SUCCESS

10 **Structured for Success** **175**
  Individual Control and System Control....................................175
  Structure Follows Strategy 178
  Integrated Model of Change 179
  Effective Leaders Are Masters of Structure..............................184
  Bibliography 185

Index...**187**

Overview Summary: The Entire Book in a Few Pages

To me, leadership implies change. Management is about maintaining the current course of action and taking corrective measures when necessary to get back on track. Leadership, on the other hand, is all about changing from the current course of action and heading in a new direction. Consequently, leadership is fundamentally about changing the behaviors of the people in the organization. With leadership, the current set of behaviors has been deemed insufficient or undesirable (by whatever means), and a new set of behaviors is needed to achieve a new set of results.

From the field of system dynamics, we know that the *structure* of an organizational system gives rise to the behavior of this system over time and, ultimately, to its performance results. Structure guides behavior, and behavior generates results. Structure includes any and all interconnections among different entities and elements of the organizational system, such as policies, procedures, budget controls, financial incentives, hierarchies of authority, employee training, inventory management processes, hiring/firing processes, and so on. Leverage for changing the performance of a system is not found in knee-jerk reactions to recent performance results or data points (e.g., layoff, excess inventory). Instead, leverage for changing the system comes from changing the underlying structures that create the behaviors that generate the current level of performance. If this maxim is applied to leadership, then effective leaders are the ones that can create the proper structures within an organization that more easily generate the desired behaviors and results. The term *structured for success* comes from this idea. Does the organization have a clear definition of what *success* is for the organization, and are the right *structures* in place to drive the actions/activities needed to create that success?

If anyone has to "fight the system" or "go around the system" to get something accomplished in an organization, this is a big red flag that the structure of the system does not naturally generate the proper behavior or course of action. The effective leader is a *master of structure* and has several advantages over traditional leadership styles. First, the leader that is a master of structure understands the influence of structures and, therefore, has a respect for these structures and the role they play in achieving the desired level of performance (e.g., Chapters 1 and 2). Second, the leader that is a master of structure has learned several techniques for analyzing structures to determine if they generate the desired behavior or not (e.g., Chapters 3, 4, 5, and 6). Third, the leader that is a master of structure has learned more advanced techniques for analyzing structures for which the resulting behaviors are not known (e.g., Chapters 7, 8, and 9). As a result, the effective leader can confidently approach any organizational situation and determine which structures are enabling the desired characteristics and which structures are inhibiting the desired characteristics. Then, for the structures that are inhibiting or preventing (or even counteracting) the desired characteristics, the effective leader has a toolset for understanding how these structures are counterproductive and how to correct them.

Note that structure is not always external to a person. Policies, processes, organizational controls, and so on are examples of structures that are *external* to employees. However, there are many structures that are *internal* to a person that come into play, also, and the effective leader needs to understand these as well (e.g., Chapter 10). External structures tend to operate by fear, and very often when the external structure or control is removed, behavior reverts to the original (undesired) behavior. Internal structures, such as motivation and belief systems, operate by choice. As a result, they are often stronger influencers of behavior than external structures and, thus, have a more permanent effect on changing behavior for an individual. Consider the example of smoking. An external control (or structure) is to tax the price of cigarettes very heavily to discourage buying cigarettes. Depending on the amount of tax, this may have an impact on the sales of cigarettes (and, presumably, the consumption of cigarettes by people). However, if taxes were lowered, sales would most likely increase, and the removal of the financial barrier to smoking would cause many previous smokers to resume smoking. Notice that the external control of high taxes did not fundamentally change the desire to smoke. In a circuitous way, it did, but only while taxes remained high. Conversely, an internal control (or structure) is to teach people about the unhealthy and undesirable consequences of smoking so that they decide, regardless of the price of cigarettes, that they do not want to smoke.

Issues arise in organizations when internal controls and external controls contradict each other. For example, an employee is told to work in a team environment, but the employee is measured and compensated on his or her ability to execute within his or her specific domain of knowledge (e.g., engineering expertise). These contradicting controls make it difficult for the employee to *do the right thing* because it is not clear what it means to *do the right thing*. The worst scenario is to put an employee in a situation in which the best action is not obvious. Effective leaders that are masters of structure work to align the internal and external structures so that both sets of structures drive the exact same behavior. In this situation, whether the employee is more driven by external controls (i.e., in psychological terms, the employee has an *external locus of control*) or more driven by internal controls (i.e., the employee has an *internal locus of control*), the behavior exhibited by that employee is the desired behavior that will lead to the desired performance results.

Book Sections Descriptions

Section I: Systems and Structure

"We cannot solve our problems with the same level of thinking that created them."

Albert Einstein

Section I contains Chapters 1 and 2. In this section, the reader is introduced to the concept of "structure" within organizational and social "systems." The term *system* is used loosely and can represent anything, such as an entire organization, a large global corporation, a wildlife ecosystem, a group of people, or a very specific issue or problem. The term *structure* is used to represent the underlying feedback loops that drive the behavior of the system. The reader will learn that there are only two types of feedback loops: positive (or reinforcing) feedback loops that drive behavior in the same direction, and negative (or balancing) feedback loops that drive behavior toward a goal. Learning how to recognize these feedback loops and the impact they have on the issue or system being analyzed is a key skill for leaders. Referencing Albert Einstein's quote at the beginning of this section, this skill allows a leader to think at a higher level than the problem or issue at hand.

Section II: Consequence Maps

Section II contains Chapters 3, 4, 5, and 6. In Section I, the reader is exposed to the concept of a consequence map. In this section, the reader is shown the methods for developing a consequence map in Chapter 3, along with some very simple consequence maps to demonstrate feedback loops in Chapters 4, 5, and 6. The purpose of this section is to share real-life examples that may be familiar to the reader.

Provided that one of the examples hits an area of experience with which the reader is familiar, the reader may gain a much deeper understanding and appreciation for the application and utility of consequence maps. The consequence map is a key tool for the leader that is the master of structure because the consequence map can show if an organization (or whatever issue or problem) is "structured for success."

The first example given in Chapter 4 digs into more details and nuances so that the reader begins to understand better how consequence maps are developed and interpreted. The next examples in Chapters 5 and 6 give some details, but not as much as Chapter 4. The purpose of Chapters 5 and 6 is to get the reader quickly through another example. If any insights to developing and interpreting consequence maps are newly revealed in these chapters, they will be discussed. However, most of the insights to the approach are highlighted in Chapter 4, and these apply to all the examples.

Section III: System Dynamics Simulation

Section III contains Chapters 7, 8, and 9. The purpose of this section is to show how consequence maps can be extended to assist with planning and management in organizations. With consequence maps, insights and information are qualitative. This is very helpful, and, in fact, it is a necessary first step. However, there is still the opportunity to go beyond this qualitative level of understanding to provide quantitative answers that can guide decisions and policies. With a consequence map, we understand that it is possible for something to happen, but we do not necessarily know *how much* of it will happen or *when* exactly it will happen. And, with consequence maps, we can explain behaviors that we have seen in the past or know about from other situations, but we cannot predict behaviors and dynamics that we have never seen before. Simulation provides these details. Furthermore, simulation provides quantification of which feedback loops dominate the system under which conditions and over which timeframes.

The approach of developing consequence maps (called *causal loop diagrams* within the system dynamics simulation field) and then developing the corresponding simulation is very common. In many cases, it is highly recommended, as will be explained in Chapter 7. This is the approach that I used when I began working in the field, and it is often the approach I still use, depending on the objective of the analysis. Early in my career, I tried to push through the consequence map (i.e., causal loop diagram) phase of the project to get to the simulation where the "real" answers could be found. I thought that the consequence map was a necessary first step, but it was not the true purpose. I was focused on the simulation phase and getting to quantification. However, while working with some organizations, notably the Department of Education and the National Institutes of Health, I realized that the consequence map itself often provided enough information for some situations. The simulations were not only unnecessary, but often they were distracting.

On some projects, all that is needed is for the organization to see the system structure. As stated in Section II with the example consequence maps, seeing the system structure can often yield solutions very quickly. And, in some cases, the answer is so obvious that there is no need to obtain quantifiable results. The organization is going to implement the solution regardless, so why bother with building a simulation that shows it will take 5 months instead of 3 months? Or, why build a simulation that shows it improves by 10% instead of 15%? The organization plans to implement the solution no matter the length of time or level of improvement. The organization knows the solution will move them in the right direction. Or, in some cases, the simulation phase is just too technical and begins to lose the attention and motivation of the participants in the organization. As a result, I began to see the utility and effectiveness of using the consequence map as a stand-alone tool for strategic planning.

However, in many situations, the consequence map points in the right direction, but the details of a simulation are necessary to decide how and when to proceed. The chapters in Section 3 walk the reader through the use of simulation for quantifying what is seen in the consequence map. The objective of showing these example simulations is to provide the reader with additional information for those situations in which the consequence map is just the first step and a valid "what-if" scenario planning tool is required to understand all the nuances of the decisions or policies that might be implemented. Sometimes, a difference between 3 months and 5 months can make a huge difference because of time constraints, or an improvement of 10% or 15% can shift the dominance of other feedback loops. For these situations, while the consequence map gives an idea of what can happen, simulations are necessary for understanding exactly what will happen under various sets of conditions that might be experienced by the organization.

Section IV: Structured for Success

Section IV only contains Chapter 10, the final chapter. In this chapter, the concepts from earlier sections are tied together to provide a model for change within an organizational or social system. The model becomes another tool for determining if an organization is *structured for success*.

Acknowledgments

I would first and foremost like to thank my wife and daughters for their support as I worked on this book but, more importantly, as I spent many hours traveling and working with organizations to develop these concepts. I know this added stress to our lives. Without their love, encouragement, and support, I would absolutely be lost.

The material in this book is the culmination of 25 years of work. The tools and techniques presented in this book evolved slowly through studying system dynamics, researching new ideas, expanding concepts, and testing ideas in the real world. Within each person, I believe there is a "book" to be written that captures some of that person's key thoughts, ideas, and experiences the person wants to pass on for the benefit of others. It might be a long book, or it might be a very short book. The content of the book has been helpful to that person, and the person wants to pass that content along in the hopes that it will have the same positive impact on others. This is my book. I strongly believe in the power and effectiveness of the tools and techniques captured here, and they are fundamental to my approach in life and work.

I would like to thank several people with whom I have been fortunate to work over the last couple of decades. These people have had a significant influence on my thought processes and accomplishments. I have put them in chronological order next.

Dr. Mildred Pryor: Dr. Pryor was an important mentor for me in my first few formative years in the working world. She was the one that sparked my interest in Total Quality Management (TQM), Lean, and Six Sigma and then fanned the flames by introducing me to other like-minded people in the workplace, providing me with unique, high-visibility opportunities that were typically unavailable to young workers, and enthusiastically supporting my work. These were the foundations that helped strengthen my inquisitive and analytical mind, which led to my interest in the field of system dynamics. Since our initial meeting, we have grown to become good colleagues, and we have written a book and several articles together.

Dr. John Sterman: Although not the inventor of system dynamics, Dr. Sterman is a key front-person for the field, and his entertaining style of presentation causes the audience (including me) to want to learn and see the world through a better lens. He was the person from whom I initially learned system dynamics at a week-long executive seminar at Massachusetts Institute of Technology (MIT) back in the early 1990s. He has offered several pieces of good advice along my journey, and I appreciate the time and attention he has given me over the years.

Dr. Louis Alfeld: I worked for Dr. Alfeld for several years at his company in Bethesda, Maryland, in the late 1990s. He was instrumental in the development of my skills in system dynamics modeling and causal loop diagram development. He was one of the first students of the inventor of system dynamics, Dr. Jay Forrester, and because of that I often felt that I was learning at the "feet of the master."

Dr. Margaret Pinder: I met Dr. Pinder when she was my instructor in a graduate course at a college in Dallas, Texas. Since that time, we have become colleagues and have worked on several projects together. I walk away from almost all of our conversations with the motivation and desire to learn more and improve the world in some unique and fascinating way. She was instrumental in one of the projects presented in this book. This is important because this project showed me how the content in this book could be used by any type of organization. She was also instrumental in the development of the leadership model presented in Chapter 10.

Robert (Bob) Sholtes: I met Bob in 1997 when I joined Dr. Alfeld's company in Bethesda, Maryland (see previous reference). Immediately, I felt like we had a strong working partnership that I had not experienced previously. We were perfectly in synch. We did some incredible work together at that company and for many more years after that. We co-authored a book together and still continue to work to push our ideas and concepts further. He is a dear friend, and I look forward to hearing his stories as he retires and begins to live life on his new catamaran.

I would also like to thank Lara Zoble at CRC Press (Taylor & Francis) for her interest in my work and the opportunity to publish this material. I appreciate her willingness to work with me to make this book a reality. I am very excited to finally see it in print. :-)

About the Author

 **J. Chris White** was born and raised in Dallas, Texas, and now resides in Rockwall, Texas, with his wife and two daughters. He holds a Bachelor of Science in aerospace engineering from MIT (1990) and a Master of Science in industrial engineering from the University of Michigan (1992). He is a senior program manager at DESE Research and was previously the president of ViaSim Solutions. In addition to these roles, he is currently an adjunct instructor at the University of Texas at Dallas (UTD). Chris has published numerous articles in the fields of leadership, TQM, Six Sigma, project management, strategic management, and simulation. He recently published *The Dynamic Progress Method: Using Advanced Simulation to Improve Project Planning and Management* (CRC Press, 2016, ISBN 9781466504370) with his colleague, Robert M. Sholtes.

Readers are encouraged to visit the Web sites associated with this book:
www.StructuredForSuccess.com
www.ConsequenceMap.com

SYSTEMS AND STRUCTURE

1

SYSTEMS AND STRUCTURE

Chapter 1

Leaders as Masters of Structure

Leaders today have a tough job. In companies, great results are demanded of the leaders, or they risk losing their jobs to others that will "get the job done." In politics, we look to leaders to solve all the problems of our city, state, or nation. In non-profits, we expect leaders to fix all the poverty, injustice, and homelessness we see in the world around us. In hospitals, we expect leaders to heal all the sick, prevent all illnesses, and cure new diseases as they are found. Those are all big expectations.

Let me first state that a *leader* can be anyone. A leader is not just the person at the top of the hierarchy. To me, a leader is anyone who produces change. I consider leadership different from management. Of course, you don't have to agree with me, and there are numerous books on both subjects. To me, leadership implies change. Management, on one hand, is about maintaining the current course of action and taking corrective measures when necessary to get back on track. Leadership, on the other hand, is all about changing from the current course of action and heading in a new direction. Consequently, leadership is fundamentally about changing the behaviors of the people in the organization. The current set of behaviors has been deemed insufficient or undesirable (by whatever means), and a new set of behaviors is needed to achieve a new set of results.

Next, let me state that the examples in the first paragraph are impossible situations. Consequently, it is impossible for leaders to succeed every time in every situation. Sure, there are some successes here and there, and occasionally there is the rare leader who can move from situation to situation and still get great results. However, in most cases, the successes are few and far between, and the successes cannot be duplicated or repeated. There are many times that a leader will get great results in one situation, but when that leader tries the same approach in a new situation, the results are very poor. I would argue that, in many cases, the successes are due in large part to plain luck, and good (perhaps not great) results would have still occurred in the absence of the specific leader. In other words, the success was due to something else, not just the leader. Why am I so sure of this? Because I have experienced it myself. On several occasions, I have been considered the "leader" for some group or initiative that performed very well, despite anything I did. The conditions were right, and the only way we were not going to succeed was if I purposely tried to sabotage the project or initiative.

I am not saying that success is impossible. I am just saying that in most cases, success is more due to luck or brute force. The leaders that are consistently successful (and remember that a leader can be anyone that produces change) are those that have the unique capability to understand the processes, policies, and controls that need to exist to enable great results. In this book, we will call this *structured for success*. The effective leader is the one who knows what *structures* need to be in place to drive behavior toward whatever has been defined as *success* (e.g., reduction of the number of people living in poverty, decrease in homelessness rate, increase in company profits). The effective leader is a *master of structure*.

A Silly Example

To set the stage for this book, a fictitious example will be used as a metaphor. Imagine a person with large dominos on each side of him, as in Figure 1.1. The person has a dilemma. He is crowded and cramped by these dominos and has nowhere to move. But, the person has an idea for how to solve his dilemma. Figure 1.2 shows this solution: push one of the dominos over so that there is more space. It makes perfect sense from his vantage point. The dominos are the reason for the cramped conditions, so removing one of the dominos will remove the constraint and create an open environment.

However, Figure 1.3 shows the "big picture" from an overhead view so that we are looking down at the top of the dominos. Surrounding the man is a circle of dominos that begins on one side of him and goes all the way around to end on the other side of him. In Figures 1.1 and 1.2, the two dominos that the person sees are actually just the first and last dominos in the chain. Of course, from this overhead view of the big picture it is now easy to see how this will play out. At first, when the man pushes over one of the dominos, he will have some free space for a while, and he will believe that he has solved his problem. Unfortunately, this open space is short-lived. The first domino will knock over the second domino, which will knock over the third domino, and so on. Eventually, the person will be struck by the last domino, which will create a much worse situation for the person than originally encountered in Figure 1.1. He will get crushed!

While this is a silly hypothetical example, it provides a great metaphor for many of the situations that we encounter in real life. Problems or issues look easy to solve

Figure 1.1   Person with a dilemma.

Figure 1.2   Person with a dilemma implementing a solution.

from our limited vantage point. To relieve the immediate "pain" or "discomfort," an action is taken to solve the problem, which might yield some benefits in the near term. Yet, over time, the problem or issue is back again in full force (or maybe even worse) in the long term, as if the problem was never solved in the first place. As a real-world "domino" example, consider the housing bubble in the 2007–08 timeframe. Because of financial pressures, mortgage companies proliferated the use of subprime mortgages in an attempt to make more money. Failures of subprime mortgages led to failures of mortgage companies (or mortgage subsidiaries of larger companies), which then impacted lenders, which then impacted homebuilders, which then impacted the U.S. economy, which eventually impacted the world economy. The initial financial "pain" felt by the mortgage companies eventually became a financial "collapse," which was much worse than the initial pain.

The Goal of This Book

Consider a few questions related to Figures 1.1 through 1.3.

- Will the person succeed in his ultimate objective?
- What is the intended consequence of the action?
- Will there be an unintended consequence to this action?
- Will the person associate the final result with the initial action?

Figure 1.3 The big picture of the person with a dilemma.

With this exaggerated example, the answers are easy. No, the person will not succeed in his ultimate objective of gaining open space. The intended consequence of the action is to create open space (which it does in the near term), but there is an unintended consequence of getting squashed by the final domino (which will happen in the long run). Finally, the person will most likely *not* associate the final result with the initial action because he does not see the full picture. He only sees two dominos, not the entire circle of dominos. Instead, since there is a long delay, he will most likely associate the final result with some other action or situation that occurred right before he was struck by the final domino (e.g., wind blowing, car honking a horn, sneeze).

What is happening in this situation? First, the person cannot see the full big picture. In other words, the person has NO VISIBILITY. Second, the person seeks to eliminate the immediate pain or discomfort in the short term, so there is NO LONG-TERM FOCUS. Third, the person will not associate the final outcome with the initial action, which results in NO LEARNING. If the situation ever happens again, and the person finds himself stuck between two dominos, the person will most likely attempt the same solution because it provided some immediate relief in the first example.

In an organization, these three problems lead to some other very interesting problems. NO VISIBILITY of the big picture creates competing *local* solutions to the same problem instead of a common *global* solution. If you can only see part of the picture, you can only solve part of the problem. Moreover, the action taken in one part of the organization to solve a problem very often creates a new problem in another part of the organization. The term *competing solutions* is used because one group's actions may nullify or limit another group's actions, since neither group "sees" the consequences of their actions on the other groups.

NO LONG-TERM FOCUS creates the attitude that the best solutions to problems are the solutions that have quick, immediate positive results. If my attention span is only a week, anything that happens next month will not be associated with something that happens this week. We are a society of immediate gratification. We want to see fast results. This holds true for our solutions to major issues and problems. If a solution does not yield immediate results, then it must not be a good solution; let's try something else.

NO LEARNING creates the belief that we need to keep doing what we are doing. That is, we need to keep applying the same solution whenever the same problem pops up. In the subprime mortgage example, that is exactly what happened. In the beginning, loans had very little risk associated with them because loans were only given to people with good credit, good ability to pay, and so on. When this did not produce enough profit for the companies, riskier loans were offered to people with less-than-good credit, a lower ability to pay, and so on. When this did not create enough profit, the same action was taken again: lower the credit required, and so forth, and take on more risk. Eventually, all the bad loans caught up with the mortgage company, and there was a multitude of defaults. Because the first action of reducing the required credit, and so on, resulted in a quick infusion of profit for the companies (and because the delay between this first action and the resulting collapse was in the order of years), this was deemed an excellent approach to the problem. Thus, when the mortgage companies found themselves in a tight financial situation again, they went back to the same solution: lower the required credit, and so forth, even lower, and take on even more risk. This is like pushing over another domino. Eventually, years later, the final domino came crashing down, and the housing bubble popped.

The goal of this book is to help the reader eliminate or minimize these three common limitations that we experience with difficult situations in organizations, in societies, and in our own lives by understanding more about system structures and how these structures enable or inhibit successful accomplishment of desired goals.

To begin with, this book will increase the reader's ability to see the big picture (which solves NO VISIBILITY), or see the full "system." A *system* is any set of entities or parts that interact or work together to accomplish some objective or function. Some easy systems to imagine are the human body, the solar system, a natural ecosystem, and a process within an organization. In each of these examples, there are multiple parts of the system: organs and cells for the human body, planets and moons for the solar system, predators and prey in the ecosystem, and tasks and resources in the organizational process. All of these parts interact together or interconnect in some form or fashion to do something. Another example of a system, which is a little harder to imagine, is a problem or issue, such as subprime mortgages, obesity, addiction, racism, or poverty. In the subprime mortgages example, the parts of the system include the companies, the salespeople, the accounts, and the clients. These all interact together. While it could be argued that they did not interact well together in the collapse, they still interacted together. This book will help the reader learn how to see the larger system instead of just a small part of the system. In addition, the reader will learn that these interactions among the entities or parts of a system form the structures of the system that enable or inhibit successful accomplishment of the desired goals.

Next, this book will increase the reader's ability to make decisions that are best for the long term (which solves NO LONG-TERM FOCUS). The reader will gain the ability to understand how a system might behave in the short term and the long term and, especially, to see how an action or decision can have a good short-term result yet have a bad long-term result. Or, conversely, the reader will gain the ability to understand that some bad short-term results may be absolutely necessary to achieve the good long-term results. Consider a daily exercise regimen. Results are not seen immediately. It takes time for muscles to develop and stamina to increase. Over the long run, results will be positive, but the exerciser has to go through some "pain" in the short term to get to the better results in the long term. The reader will see that this is true for many problems, issues, processes, and systems.

Last, this book will increase the reader's learning and intuition about how systems behave so that the reader can make better decisions (which solves NO LEARNING). In many situations, our "learning" is limited by our blindness to the other interacting parts of the system. Whatever we do, it can only be a partial solution, at best, because we know nothing of the rest of the system. We do not know if our actions are helpful to the other parts of the system or detrimental to the other parts of the system. Our "learning feedback loop" is very limited. If a child touches a hot stove, the child will learn immediately that touching a hot stove causes pain. To avoid the pain, the child will learn not to touch a hot stove. This is because the "learning feedback loop" is immediate. As soon as the child touches the hot stove, the finger that touched the stove feels the pain. Yet, imagine if a child touched a hot stove and the pain was felt 2 hours later in the big toe of one of the child's feet. The child would never associate the touching of the hot stove with a finger with the pain in a big toe much later. Instead, the child would associate the pain in the big toe with something that happened right before the pain was experienced (e.g., walking through a door, putting on a shoe, stepping on a rock).

This is what usually happens in complex systems: an action (cause) and its associated consequence (effect) are significantly separated instead of tightly linked. It becomes impossible to "learn" how the system operates and strengthen our intuition in this type of situation. And, if we cannot learn how the system operates, we cannot understand the system well enough to make the best decisions, take the best actions, or institute the best policies.

How are these limitations corrected? We will focus on three new perspectives.

Moving from SNAPSHOTS to PATTERNS

The first perspective that needs to change is for us to move from focusing on single snapshots in time to focusing on patterns of behavior. Figure 1.4 provides a graphic to help with this notion. The graph in Figure 1.4 shows an activity over

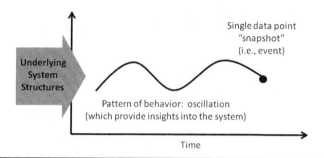

Figure 1.4 Moving from SNAPSHOTS to PATTERNS. (From White, J. Chris and Sholtes, Robert M., *The Dynamic Progress Method: Using Advanced Simulation to Improve Project Planning and Management,* **CRC Press, 2016, figure 3.4. With permission.)**

time (moving left to right). At the far right, we see a single point that is highlighted. This represents the single snapshot. Typically, we see a single data point (e.g., stock-out of inventory, layoff, missed sales opportunity), and we make knee-jerk reactions to that single data point. Yet, as can be seen in Figure 1.4, there is a pattern of behavior that precedes the single data point. In this example, it is an oscillatory behavior (i.e., fluctuating). Looking at this oscillatory pattern, it is conceivable that the data will eventually trend upward again since that is what it has done in the past. In other words, if we let the system continue to operate with no intrusions or changes, the behavior will likely correct itself. By looking at the pattern of behavior that precedes the single data point, we may decide not to interfere. However, by only focusing on the single data point, we may feel the need to react strongly. Looking at the single data point is a short-term view, while looking at the pattern of behavior is a longer-term view. Managing a system based on the pattern of behavior (and not the single data point) creates patience and the confidence that things will eventually change.

At the far left of Figure 1.4 is a large arrow that states that there are underlying system structures that generate the pattern of behavior, which leads to the single data point. A good analogy for this is a giant wave pool at a water park. Imagine standing at the shallow end of the wave pool. The single data point is where the water touches your legs. At one moment, the water touches your leg up at your knees. The next moment the water is down to your ankles. Then the water is back up at your knees again, and so on. These are single data points. Depending on when we take the snapshot picture, the water is at a different place on our legs. As we back up and look at the larger picture, we see waves coming. In fact, we can even see a wave off in the distance that will eventually result in a single data point of the water touching our knees. We can also see the low points between the waves that will eventually result in a single data point of the water touching our ankles. Finally, if we step back even further, we can see that there is a machine behind a wall that generates these large waves. The wave-generating machine is the structure of the

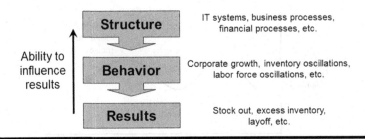

Figure 1.5 Structure drives results. (From White, J. Chris and Sholtes, Robert M., *The Dynamic Progress Method: Using Advanced Simulation to Improve Project Planning and Management,* **CRC Press, 2016, figure 3.3. With permission.)**

system that is creating the oscillating patterns of waves that result in the single data points of the water touching our knees and ankles. In Chapter 2, the reader will learn more about what constitutes the structure of a system.

Figure 1.5 captures the graphic from Figure 1.4 in a slightly different manner. Starting at the top, Figure 1.5 shows that the structure of the system (i.e., the various business processes, systems, policies, etc.) generates the patterns of behavior that are seen over time for the system (i.e., the oscillations in inventory or the workforce), and these behaviors create the individual snapshot output results that are measured for each time period (i.e., the stock-out of material).

A key item to note in Figure 1.5 is the arrow on the far left. The arrow indicates that our ability to influence the behavior and results of the system in the long term lie in changing the underlying system structures, not knee-jerk reacting to the single data snapshots (which is a short-term approach). At the level of the single snapshots of data, the system has "momentum" that prevents our actions from having much effect. Consider the wave pool example again. The water coming toward us in waves has mass and momentum. We cannot just hold up our hands to stop the water. In fact, sometimes the oncoming water is so strong it can sweep our feet out from under us so that we lose our balance and fall down. The same is true of organizational, social, political, and other systems. The built-up momentum of the system is difficult, if not impossible, to stop immediately with a knee-jerk reaction to a single data point. We may have a small, short-term positive result, but the system will eventually push us over or knock us down like the wave pool or dominos examples.

Moving from LINES to LOOPS

After moving from reactions to single SNAPSHOTS of data to looking at the PATTERNS of behavior of the system, the next perspective we need to change is to move from straight LINES of cause and effect to feedback LOOPS. Figure 1.6 provides a simple example of this. Instead of seeing causes and effects as a long chain,

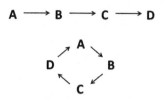

Figure 1.6 Moving from LINES of cause and effect to feedback LOOPS.

we need to understand that these long chains eventually come back around to close on themselves. Thus, instead of a situation in which A causes B and B causes C and C causes D, we may have a situation in which A causes B and B causes C and C causes D, which comes back around again to influence A. Imagine walking on the moon. If you started at one point and just walked straight in one direction, eventually you would circumvent the moon and end up at the exact same starting point. Your straight line just became a loop. This concept may not make complete sense now, but Chapters 2 and 3 will show more details behind this notion.

Moving from ONE to MANY

Once we get to the point that we are see ONE feedback loop of cause and effect instead of just a straight-line chain of cause and effect, we need to gain the perspective that there are always MANY feedback loops within a system. Rarely is there ever just a single feedback loop. Chapters 2 and 3 will go into more details of this concept, but for now the reader needs to appreciate that there are usually several feedback loops that interconnect and interact together in a complex system. Figure 1.7 shows this concept. In Figure 1.7, imagine being part of the feedback loop ABCD. Suppose we see a problem with C, and we implement a solution at C. In this graphic, the reader can see that C is also part of the feedback loops that involve HI and BEFG. Thus, taking action at C will most likely have ripple effects and unintended consequences in these other two feedback loops, which may come back to have some other impact on C later in time. Who knows?

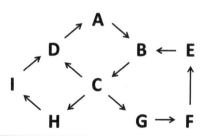

Figure 1.7 Moving from ONE feedback loop to MANY.

Why Does This Matter?

These new perspectives matter because the systems we deal with on a daily basis in organizations and societies are very complex. "Complex" means that the systems have a multitude of parts or entities and numerous interconnections or interdependencies among those parts or entities. As the amount of interdependencies increases, the likelihood that an action will generate *unintended consequences* also increases due to the connections with other parts of the system. And, the more unintended consequences that are generated, the less likelihood that an action will generate its *intended consequence.*

In essence, complex systems, due to all the interdependencies, behave opposite to our intuition. Their behaviors are counterintuitive. This is horrible, because it means that the actions that we naturally want to take are typically the *exact opposite* of the actions that need to be taken. Suppose you took your car to a mechanic. When you got your car back, the steering system had accidentally been reversed. Now, when you turn left, the car goes right. And, when you turn right, the car goes left. You would surely have a wreck within minutes of driving this type of car. The steering is exactly the opposite of what your intuition and natural reactions want to do based on your many years of driving experience. Your "muscle memory" reactively turns right to make the car turn right, which is the absolute wrong thing to do in this case. Our intuition causes us to take actions that may not help, may cause other problems, or may make the original problem even worse. As such, we often cause our own problems!

Dr. Jay Forrester, the inventor of the system dynamics modeling and simulation methodology, states this phenomenon with a few insights. First, complex systems show different behaviors and consequences in the short term and the long term for an implemented policy, decision, or action. What is good in the short term typically results in poor long-term performance. Conversely, what is good in the long term typically results in poor short-term performance. Thus, when leaders tend to focus on short-term results, they are missing the better long-term results. Leaders need to understand that there often has to be discipline in the short term to withstand the poor short-term results or "pain" in favor of the long-term positive results.

Next, our intuition and limited knowledge of system structures usually cause us to implement decisions, policies, or actions in the parts of the system in which they are least effective. Dr. Forrester uses the term *leverage*. We tend to implement changes in the parts of the system that have the least leverage for changing the behavior of the system. Along those lines, even if we happen to find the parts of the system that have high leverage for changing the behavior of the system, our intuition and limited knowledge of system structures usually cause us to make the change in the *wrong direction*. In other words, we make a change to increase something when the better decision is to decrease that something. As a result, we have two strikes against us: we tend to pick the areas of the system with least leverage, or we pick an area with high leverage and we move the needle in the opposite direction of optimal.

With a limited view of the system, we only understand the parts or elements of the system that we are involved with, but not the total system with all its interactions, interconnections, and interdependencies (i.e., system structure). Without an understanding of this structure, it is impossible to know the true consequences that decisions, policies, and actions will have in the short term and the long term. And, without an understanding of true consequences, our best intentions often lead to extremely poor results because the overall behavior of complex systems is counterintuitive, and we typically implement changes where they have the least probability of success.

By making the leader a master of structure, the hope is to reduce the unintended consequences of our actions and increase the intended consequences of our actions. In Chapter 2 on feedback loops, the leader will gain a better understanding of the interdependencies (structure) within and among the parts of a system. In Chapter 3 on consequence maps, the leader will learn a framework and methodology for communicating about these interdependencies and determining their resulting behaviors. With consequence maps, the leader will increase his or her ability to generate intended consequences and minimize the generation of unintended consequences.

Bibliography

Deming, W. Edwards, *Out of the Crisis*, Cambridge, MA: MIT Press, 1982.

Forrester, Jay W., *Industrial Dynamics*, Cambridge, MA: Productivity Press, 1961.

Forrester, Jay W., *Collected Papers of Jay W. Forrester*, Cambridge, MA: Wright-Allen Press, 1975.

Senge, Peter M., *The Fifth Discipline: The Art & Practice of the Learning Organization*, New York: Doubleday/Currency, 1990.

White, J. Chris and Sholtes, Robert M., *The Dynamic Progress Method: Using Advanced Simulation to Improve Project Planning and Management*, Boca Raton, FL: CRC Press, 2016.

Chapter 2

Feedback Loops as System Structure

Chapter 1 introduced the idea that a single organization, a group of companies, an issue, or a problem can be considered a system. Of course, the purpose of this book is to introduce a better way of understanding what happens in a system using consequence maps. A system is any group of entities, elements, or parts that are interconnected to perform a function or activity (or multiple functions or activities). This is important because it helps the effective leader immediately understand that a big-picture, systemic view is required to lead an organization, initiate a major change within an organization, or solve an important, yet very complex, issue or problem. The effective leader cannot be myopic and focus on only a few parts of the overall system. Undoubtedly, that type of approach will lead to a less-than-optimal solution. In fact, in most cases, it can actually make the situation worse. When not using a full system perspective, it is usually the case that the exact solution applied in the beginning to the situation eventually, in the long term, becomes a contributor to the original situation, problem, or issue. We will see examples of this phenomenon in later chapters that discuss specific consequence maps.

When the term *structure* is used in this book with regard to organizational, managerial, or social systems, the word points to feedback loops. In any system, the structure of the system (i.e., the underlying feedback loops) guides the behavior of the system. Thus, to be an effective leader who desires to drive change within an organization, one must know what constitutes the system structure to know how to manipulate it. Fortunately, when it comes to feedback loops, there are only two types:

1. *Positive* feedback loop (also called a *reinforcing* feedback loop)
2. *Negative* feedback loop (also called a *balancing* feedback loop)

That's it. Sounds easy, doesn't it? In one sense, it is easy. If you learn how these two types of feedback loops act, then you have the basis for the building blocks of system structure, which also means that you have the starting points for creating consequence maps. However, things get complicated very quickly when multiple feedback loops are connected and interact together. We will begin with a discussion of each type of individual feedback loop.

Positive (Reinforcing) Feedback Loop

The first feedback loop to be introduced is the positive feedback loop, also called a reinforcing feedback loop. If you have ever heard the term "vicious cycle" (or "virtuous cycle"), it is a reference to a positive (reinforcing) feedback loop. Vicious cycles work in the direction counter to your desire. For example, the vicious loop drives performance down to a lower level (i.e., worse) when you may want that performance to go up to a higher level (i.e., better). Virtuous cycles are the same thing, but they are going in the direction that you desire. For instance, the virtuous loop drives performance to a higher level (i.e., better) when you may want performance to go up to a higher level. The mechanics of the positive (reinforcing) feedback loop are such that all the elements in the feedback loop work in a way that pushes change in the same direction as the initial action. So, lower performance leads to even lower performance, or higher performance leads to even higher performance. Bad leads to worse (vicious cycle), or good leads to better (virtuous cycle).

We will start with two simple examples of positive (reinforcing) feedback loops. The first is the balance of a bank account (Figure 2.1). Assuming there are no withdrawals from the bank account, the balance of the bank account will grow in a pattern that looks like the graph on the right side of Figure 2.1. This is called exponential growth. The left side of Figure 2.1 shows how this occurs. We begin with the *Account Balance* (e.g., $100). After a period of time (e.g., 1 year) called the

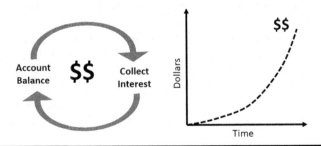

Figure 2.1   Bank account example.

compounding period, interest is collected based on some defined interest rate (e.g., 10%). Thus, for an initial balance of $100 with a compounding period of 1 year and an interest rate of 10%, the *Account Balance* at the end of Year 1 would be $110: $100 (initial balance) + $10 (10% interest on $100). Assuming no withdrawals occur, the *Account Balance* at the end of Year 2 would be $121: $110 (balance at the end of Year 1) + $11 (10% interest on $110).

Notice that that interest for Year 1 is $10, and the interest for Year 2 is $11. The interest for Year 2 is higher than the interest for Year 1. This makes sense because the balance at the end of Year 1 is higher than the initial balance (at Year 0). However, each year (assuming no withdrawals from the account) the amount of interest is larger because the balance for which the interest is collected is larger (Figure 2.2). For instance, the interest at the end of Year 3 would be $12.10, which is 10% of $121 (balance at the end of Year 2). The rightmost column in Figure 2.2 shows the difference between the amounts of interest for two successive years. Notice that this difference continues to grow and get larger. The difference between the interest collected in Year 1 and Year 2 is only $1, but the difference between the interest collected in Year 4 and Year 5 is $1.46. The growth in the amount of interest added back into the *Account Balance* each year is what drives the exponential curve. For each successive time period, the difference in value from the current time period to the previous time period grows larger, which pushes the curve to a steeper slope and gives the exponential curve that we see on the right side of Figure 2.1.

If money is not your thing, consider a second example: the population of rabbits in a large meadow (Figure 2.3). Suppose we have a field with 100 rabbits (i.e., initial *Rabbit Population* = 100). Assume that 10% of the *Rabbit Population* is capable of giving birth to baby rabbits. That is, 10% of the *Rabbit Population* are females of appropriate maturity. In this simple example, we will assume that there are plenty of male rabbits of the appropriate maturity level, also. We will also assume that a female rabbit is capable of producing a litter of one single rabbit every year. Of course, in real life, rabbit litters can be more than a single rabbit, and females may produce more than one litter per year. And, in real life, there are predators that eat the rabbits, so the population may decrease, but for this example we will assume no predators here. In Year 1, if 10% of the *Rabbit Population* (10 rabbits) give birth to a single rabbit, there will be 10 *Rabbit Births* in Year 1, or 10% of the

Time Period	Account Balance	Interest	Difference in Interest
0	$ 100.00	$ 10.00	
1	$ 110.00	$ 11.00	$ 1.00
2	$ 121.00	$ 12.10	$ 1.10
3	$ 133.10	$ 13.31	$ 1.21
4	$ 146.41	$ 14.64	$ 1.33
5	$ 161.05	$ 16.11	$ 1.46

Figure 2.2   Bank account example with specific values.

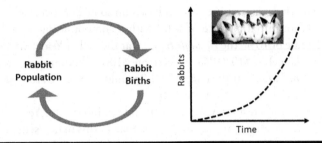

Figure 2.3 Rabbit population example.

population. With these very similar values, the reader can probably see that this is very similar to the bank balance example. As a result, this type of ecosystem would produce the same type of exponential curve for the growth of the *Rabbit Population* (Figure 2.3).

In both examples, there is an accumulation of something: dollars in the *Account Balance* or rabbits in the *Rabbit Population*. And, in both examples, for each time period there is change to the amount of things in the accumulation. In these particular examples, the change for each time period increases each time period to produce the exponential curves we see in Figures 2.1 and 2.3. A simple view of this dynamic is shown in Figure 2.4. The *State of System* is the accumulation of something. This is often called a *stock* or *level*. It represents a sort of "bucket" of something. In the field of dynamic systems, the *state* of a system is a variable that is capable of increasing and decreasing in value. Based on the value of the *State of System* (i.e., the number of items in the bucket, stock, or level), a resulting change occurs that results in an increase or decrease of the value of the *State of System*. This change is captured on the right side of Figure 2.4 as the *Change in State*. The resulting dynamic is that the *State of System* drives the *Change in State*, which comes back around to drive the *State of System*, which then drives the *Change in State* again, and so on. This is called a feedback loop. When it is drawn as it is in Figure 2.4 with + signs, it is in the form of a consequence map.

In the two examples, both feedback loops show growth (increases in values), so perhaps this could be considered the virtuous cycle in which the situation gets better and better compared to our desired outcome (e.g., more money, which is what we want). However, this same dynamic can occur in the opposite direction: a

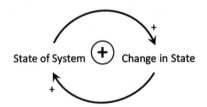

Figure 2.4 Positive feedback loop dynamics.

smaller value of *State of System* can lead to a smaller value of *Change in State*, and a smaller value of *Change in State* can then lead to a smaller value of *State of System*, and so on. Consider the melting rate of an ice cube. At first, the ice cube is very cold, so only a little ice melts to become water. This little bit of water causes the temperature of the ice cube to drop a little bit more, so even more ice melts in the next time period, and so on. This could be considered the vicious cycle in which the situation gets worse and worse compared to our desired outcome (e.g., we get less items when we want more items).

The key thing to notice is that change always occurs in the same direction. Either the changes grow and grow over time to increase the overall state value, or the changes grow and grow over time to decrease the overall state value. In Figure 2.4, this is represented by the + signs at the ends of the arrows. The direction of the arrows show the direction of cause and effect. The *State of System* drives the *Change of State* (represented by the arrow on the top of Figure 2.4), and the *Change of State* drives the *State of System* (represented by the arrow on the bottom of Figure 2.4). The + at the arrowheads indicates that the direction of change from the variable at the tail of the arrow to the variable at the head of the arrow is the same. As we saw in the bank and rabbit examples, the *State of System* causes an increase in the *Change of State*, and the *Change of State* causes an increase in the *State of System*. Or, as with the melting ice cube example, the *State of System* causes a decrease in the *Change of State*, and the *Change of State* causes a decrease in the *State of System*.

Do not interpret the + sign as "adding." In some examples, the feedback loop increase the values, but in some examples the feedback loop decreases the values. Instead, think of the + sign as meaning "change in the same direction." In a similar way, do not consider a "positive" feedback loop as a loop that increases the values. "Positive" just means that all changes are in the same direction. That is why the term "reinforcing" is often used, because a change in value reinforces a similar change in value. In Figure 2.4, a large + is put in the middle of the feedback loop to indicate this is a positive feedback loop. Figure 2.5 shows a similar method for showing the positive feedback loop. Instead of using + signs, an S is used at the arrowhead to represent the change in the *same* direction, and an R is placed in the middle of the feedback loop to indicate the *reinforcing* loop. The use of Ss and R in Figure 2.5 is another technique used for consequence maps.

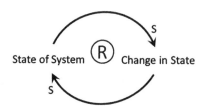

Figure 2.5   **Reinforcing feedback loop dynamics.**

Negative (Balancing) Feedback Loop

Now that the reader sees how a positive feedback loop works, the primary difference between a positive feedback loop and a negative feedback loop is that the positive feedback loop drives changes in state value in the *same* direction, and the negative feedback loop drives changes in state value in the *opposite* direction.

Figure 2.6 provides a simple example of a negative (balancing) feedback loop for pouring water into a glass. Suppose the goal is to fill a glass with water without overflowing the glass. At the start, when the glass is completely empty, the difference between the current level of water in the glass (which is 0) and the goal of a full glass (e.g., 8 ounces) is very large (i.e., 8 ounces at the beginning). As water accumulates in the glass, the difference between the current level of water in the glass and the goal of a full glass gets smaller and smaller. For example, when the glass is half full (or half empty, if you're a pessimist), the difference is 4 ounces in this particular example. Eventually, as the level of water in the glass gets closer and closer to the top of the glass, the typical reaction is to slow down the rate at which water is poured into the glass so that there is no overflow. By the end, when the goal is finally reached, the rate of pouring slows down to 0 (i.e., no more pouring when the water level is at the top of the glass). This dynamic behavior is shown in the graph on the right side of Figure 2.6. At the beginning when there is no water in the glass, the rate of pouring is at its highest so the level of water changes significantly. The steep angle of the curve near the origin of the graph in Figure 2.6 shows this. As the level of water approaches the goal (top of the glass), the rate of pouring slows down so that the change in the level of water is smaller and smaller. The shallow angle of the curve on the right side of the graph in Figure 2.6 shows this.

The consequence map on the left side of Figure 2.6 captures the mechanics that are covered in the previous paragraph. There is a *Target level* (i.e., top of the glass, 8 ounces). Based on the *Level of water in glass* compared to the *Target level*, there is a *Gap*. For instance, if the glass is empty the *Gap* is 8 ounces. When the glass has 2 ounces of water in it, the *Gap* is 6 ounces (i.e., 8 oz – 2 oz = 6 oz). As the reader learned in the previous section on positive feedback loops, the + sign at the head of an arrow indicates that a change in the variable at the tail of the arrow will cause a

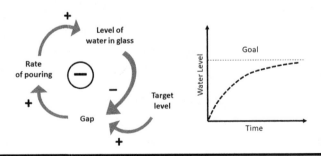

Figure 2.6   Water level example.

change in the *same* direction for the variable at the head of the arrow. Conversely, a – sign at the head of the arrow indicates that a change in the variable at the tail of the arrow will cause a change in the *opposite* direction for the variable at the head of the arrow. If the *Gap* is considered to be the difference between the *Target level* and the *Level of water in glass*, then we have the following:

$$Gap = Target\ level - Level\ of\ water\ in\ glass$$

The arrow from *Target level* to *Gap* has a + on the arrowhead to indicate that an *increase* in the *Target level* will produce an *increase* in the *Gap* (assuming everything else stays the same). However, the arrow from *Level of water in glass* to *Gap* has a – sign to indicate that an *increase* in the *Level of water in glass* will produce a *decrease* in the *Gap* (i.e., as the water level rises, the *Gap* gets smaller). For example, when the *Level of water in glass* is low (e.g., 2 oz), the *Gap* is high (e.g., 6 oz). But, when then *Level of water in glass* is higher (e.g., 7 oz), the *Gap* is smaller (e.g., 1 oz).

The *Gap* then drives a change in the system through the *Rate of pouring*. There is a + sign on the arrowhead from *Gap* to *Rate of pouring* to indicate that the *Rate of pouring* is proportional to the *Gap*. When the *Gap* is large, the *Rate of pouring* is high (fast). When the *Gap* is small, the *Rate of pouring* is low (slow). The two variables move in the same direction. Next, the *Rate of pouring* impacts the *Level of water in glass* because water is added to the glass. There is a + sign on the arrowhead from *Rate of pouring* to *Level of water in glass* to indicate that the *Level of water in glass* increases proportionally to the *Rate of pouring*. When the *Rate of pouring* is high (fast), the *Level of water in glass* changes a lot. When the *Rate of pouring* is low (slow), the *Level of water in glass* changes only a little bit. Finally, the *Level of water in glass* comes back around again to impact the *Gap*. As discussed, the – sign on the arrowhead from *Level of water in glass* to *Gap* indicates that these two variables move in the opposite direction. When the *Level of water in glass* is low, the *Gap* is high (large). When the *Level of water in glass* is high, the *Gap* is low (small).

Another example of a negative (balancing) feedback loop is the reaction of our body when we are cold (Figure 2.7). Our body has a *Target value* temperature of 98.6 °F. Based on our current *Body temperature*, there is a *Gap*. In response to the *Gap*, we *Shiver* to generate warmth for our body and to increase our *Body temperature*, which closes the *Gap*. When we are really cold, we tend to *Shiver* a lot. But, as our *Body temperature* approaches the natural *Target value* of 98.6 °F for our bodies, the *Gap* decreases and we tend to *Shiver* less and less. When our *Body temperature* is the same as the *Target value* of 98.6 °F, the shivering stops because we have reached our goal. This behavior is shown in the graph on the right side of Figure 2.7. Notice that the consequence map and graph in Figure 2.7 look exactly like the diagram and graph in Figure 2.7.

Figure 2.8 shows the general representation of a negative (balancing) feedback loop as a consequence map. There is a *Gap* between the *Desired Goal* of the system and the current *State of System*, which drives a *Change in State* to decrease the

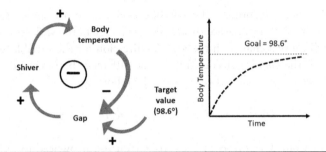

Figure 2.7   Body temperature example.

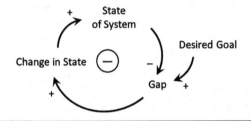

Figure 2.8   Negative feedback loop dynamics.

Gap and reach the *Desired Goal*. The reason we can say that the negative feedback loop drives change in the *opposite* direction (as compared to the positive feedback loop that drives change in the *same* direction) is because the negative feedback loop works to decrease the *Gap* (instead of increase it). As with the positive feedback loop that can drive increases in value or decreases in value, the negative feedback loop can act to drive the *State of System* to increase to close the *Gap*, or it can act to drive the *State of System* to decrease to close the *Gap*. For instance, consider the body temperature example in Figure 2.7 again. When we are cold, the body temperature is lower than the desired goal, and our bodies shiver to increase the body temperature. However, when we are hot, the body temperature is higher than the desired goal, and our bodies sweat to decrease the body temperature down to the desired goal. The hotter we are, the more we sweat. When we are not very hot, we do not sweat very much. The similarity is that the negative feedback loop drives big changes when the gap is large and smaller changes when the gap is small (no matter what the direction of the change). In other words, the changes shrink over time. Yet, with the positive feedback loop, the changes grow over time.

Figure 2.9 shows the same structure and consequence map as Figure 2.8 except it uses the S for changes in the same direction (instead of the + sign) and O for changes in the opposite direction (instead of the − sign). The negative feedback loop is also called a balancing feedback loop (B) because the system attempts to reach a "balanced" state in which the *State of System* is the same as the *Desired Goal* of the system. When the *State of System* is higher than the *Desired Goal*, the

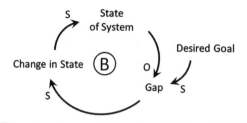

Figure 2.9 Balancing feedback loop dynamics.

system works to decrease the *State of System* down to the *Desired Goal*. And, when the *State of System* is lower than the *Desired Goal*, the system works to increase the *State of System* up to the *Desired Goal*. Furthermore, over time the magnitude of the changes tend to shrink (assuming the *Desired Goal* remains the same).

By themselves, the positive (reinforcing) feedback loop and the negative (balancing) feedback loop are not difficult to understand. The examples provided are very simple, but so are the dynamic behaviors of these two fundamental system structures. The term "dynamic behaviors" is used to indicate that the behaviors change over time. For the positive feedback loop, the changes tend to grow over time. But, for the negative feedback loop, the changes tend to shrink over time. Complexity and difficulties arise when multiple feedback loops are interconnected.

Combinations of Feedback Loops and the Common S-Curve

Let us first consider the easiest combination of feedback loops, the simple S-curve, which is a combination of a single positive feedback loop and a single negative feedback loop in the same consequence map. The reader is most likely very familiar with the concept of the S-curve: there is a growth of something (e.g., market share for a new product), which eventually slows down (e.g., the market is saturated so the market share for the new product reaches a maximum). Sometimes, the S-curve is followed by a decline, but we will not discuss that behavior at this time. We will only focus on the initial accelerated growth and decreasing growth: the S. Figure 2.10 shows the typical S-curve. Notice the quick growth in the beginning (left) with a slower growth at the end that perhaps even flattens out (right).

The structure of the system that generates S-curve behavior is shown in the consequence map in Figure 2.11. The system is a combination of a positive feedback loop (shown on the left) and a negative feedback loop (shown on the right). The variable that is shared between the two feedback loops is the *State of System*. For consistency, the variable *Change in State* remains with the same wording. However, the *Change in State* action for the positive feedback loop will be different from the *Change in State* action for the negative feedback loop. The wording is kept

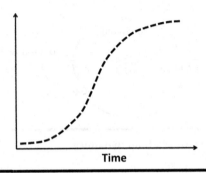

Figure 2.10 Typical S-curve behavior.

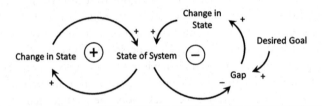

Figure 2.11 Typical S-curve feedback loop structure.

from Figure 2.4 (for the positive feedback loop) and Figure 2.8 (for the negative feedback loop) to allow the reader to see the same loops. Because *State of System* is shared between the two loops in the consequence map, it becomes immediately obvious that the *State of System* is going to be in flux (or at least change a little) as each feedback loop tries to alter it.

If the S-curve consequence map is composed of a positive feedback loop and a negative feedback loop, as indicated in Figure 2.11, it makes sense to look at the individual behavior of each loop. The left side of Figure 2.12 is a duplication of the exponential curve on the right side of Figure 2.1, which is the resulting dynamic behavior of a positive (reinforcing) feedback loop. The right side of Figure 2.12 is a duplication of the curve on the right side of Figure 2.6, which is the resulting dynamic behavior of a negative (balancing) feedback loop that is seeking a "goal." Figure 2.13 pulls these two graphs together in a way that creates the S-shape. Figure 2.14 is that same as Figure 2.13 but with the axes removed so that only the S-curve remains with the feedback loop designations).

As shown in Figure 2.14, the dynamic behavior of the S-curve is a combination of a positive feedback loop and a negative feedback loop. In Figure 2.14, it may appear as though the positive feedback loop happens first, and then the negative feedback loop happens. That is not the case at all. In reality, both feedback loops are always operating. Instead, there is tendency for a particular feedback loop to *dominate* the behavior and performance of the system at a particular period of time based on the parameters can conditions that exist.

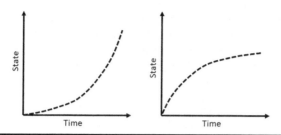

Figure 2.12 Positive feedback loop behavior (left) and negative feedback loop behavior (right).

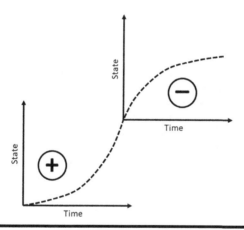

Figure 2.13 Combination of positive feedback loop and negative feedback loop behaviors.

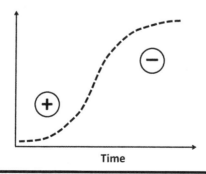

Figure 2.14 Typical S-curve behavior due to structure of feedback loops.

Consider the introduction of a new product by a company as an example. The phenomenon begins when the new product or technology (e.g., microwave ovens, DVD players, MP3 players) is released to the public by the company. In the beginning, the novelty of the technology and its new capabilities attracts a small set of customers. At this time, the price of the new technology may be high, but there will usually be a small set of customers that are both interested in the new technology and have enough money to buy it. This kicks off the positive feedback loop. This small set of customers is like the account balance in Figure 2.1 or the rabbit population in Figure 2.3. This small set of customers represents only a tiny fraction of the overall market, so it is not enough to cause any significant changes in the vast world market. This small set of customers talks to their friends and evangelizes about how wonderful and convenient the new product or technology is. As a result, a few more people become customers. Now, the set of customers has some momentum as word of mouth spreads. As more products are purchased, the company now has more money to devote to marketing and advertising to generate even more customers. Typically, at this point sales are enough to begin to drop the price of the new technology, which attracts even more customers. This is the positive feedback loop working in full force. The state of the system is such that there are no limiting factors (negative feedback loops): this set of customers is still small compared to the overall market, and this new product or technology is still the only one on the market.

As the set of customers continues to grow, a few other companies will usually take notice and make the move to enter the market. Now there is competition. With competition comes price wars, advertising battles, and so on. The initial company that released the new technology is still gaining customers, but many other potential customers are going to the competitors instead. Thus, the rate of growth of the customer base begins to slow down as more and more competitors enter the market and price wars cause prices to drop so that profits are reduced. This is the negative feedback loop kicking in. With less profits, there is less marketing and advertising, and so on, and the rate of growth of the customer base for this company begins to slow down even more. Now, the negative feedback loop is in full swing, and the number of customers begins to settle down at a level that is sustainable by the market with its new competitors and new prices. The state of the system is such that the limiting factors are stronger than the growth factors.

As another example, consider the growth of a population of rabbits in a large meadow. In Figure 2.3, it appears that the rabbit population will continue to grow forever. That is not the case. Eventually, the rabbit population would experience some limiting factors (i.e., negative feedback loops). For instance, the rabbits require food (e.g., grass) to eat. Suppose the large meadow is covered with grass. In the beginning, there is plenty of grass for the rabbits to eat. The rabbits eat the grass, and the grass has sufficient time to grow back. There is more than enough grass for everyone, so the rabbit population thrives (positive feedback loop). If there is a spot in the meadow with no grass because a bunch of rabbits just nibbled it all up, there is plenty of grass elsewhere in the meadow for the rabbits to eat while the bare patch grows back over the next few weeks. But, as the rabbit population doubles in size, and then doubles in size again, and so on, the conditions are such that less and less grass (food) is available for all the rabbits. And, the grass that is eaten does not have sufficient time to grow back to become a food source again. If there are too many rabbits compared to the amount of grass, some of the rabbits will starve to death due to lack of food. Eventually, the grass will act as the "balancing" element for the rabbit population (negative feedback loop). If there are fewer rabbits compared to the amount of grass, the rabbit population keeps growing. But, when there are more rabbits compared to the amount grass, rabbits die off to bring the rabbit population back down over time to the level where the amount of grass is sufficient. Hence, the rabbit population will eventually settle at a level that matches the meadow's ability to grow grass and feed the rabbits.

As an extreme example, imagine a small field that is 10 yards by 10 yards (100 square yards). In this system of rabbits and grass, both feedback loops always operate. It is just that the conditions in the beginning (i.e., few rabbits, lots of grass) are such that the effects of the negative feedback loop are not a limiting factor. Eventually, as the rabbit population grows, the negative feedback loop driven by the growth of grass overwhelms the growth of the population (which is still happening from the positive feedback loop) and slows its growth accordingly. This is why natural ecosystems can be severely impacted by hunting policies, building dams, and so forth. In the case of hunting, if too many predators (e.g., wolves, coyotes) are removed from the ecosystem, the balancing mechanism for the populations of smaller animals (e.g., squirrels, rabbits) is removed, so these smaller animals thrive. When the smaller animals thrive, the larger populations eat more food (e.g., grass, bushes) so that a particular ecosystem can become so bare that the animals have to migrate to some other ecosystem to survive (which, of course, then causes balance issues in the new ecosystem, etc.).

The reader can probably imagine many other examples, such as the housing crisis of the 2000s, the Internet tech company bubble of the 1990s, the rise of MTV in the 1980s, and so on. Any time that there is rapid growth in a system, keep an eye out for the possible limiting factors that will eventually constrain the growth to create the S-curve. There are always limits to growth. Unfortunately, nothing goes on forever. A difficult aspect of this change in behavior from growth (due to the positive feedback loop) to stagnation (due to the negative feedback loop) is that decisions, actions, or policies that generate wonderful results in the initial short term (e.g., exponential growth) do not necessarily translate into wonderful results in the long term. For instance, advertising may be a key activity to generating sales for a new technology, but continued advertising will most likely not be enough to overcome the stagnation and balancing forces of market share, new competitors, and so forth. At that point, the best action is to introduce another new technology to create another growth portion of the S-curve.

Combinations of Multiple Feedback Loops and Resulting Behaviors

The purpose for understanding the behaviors of positive and negative feedback loops is to help leaders gain insight into the systems that they are managing and controlling. Often, a consequence mapping exercise begins by observing the behavior of a few key elements in the system (i.e., key metrics). From the descriptions in this chapter, the effective leader will be able to associate observed behaviors with the underlying feedback loops that generate those behaviors. The purpose of consequence mapping is to capture these feedback loops graphically to see how they interconnect and interact to create the behavior of the system. By knowing which feedback loop structures create which system behaviors, the effective leader will have a good starting point for the consequence mapping exercise (which will be covered in Chapter 3).

The author will admit up front that, in many cases, the output behavior from a system does not lend itself well to interpretation of feedback loops because of the interaction of many feedback loops (which causes some "cancellation" effects). Some loops are pushing the system in one direction while other loops are pushing the system in the opposite direction, and the strengths of these feedback loops are relatively the same, so the net effect is "no change" even though there may be quite a lot of interaction occurring.

Yet, there are some instances in which the behavior shown by a system is very indicative of the underlying feedback loops. The previous section on the common S-curve is a great example. A positive (reinforcing) feedback loop clearly dominates the system in the short term. Then, the loop dominance shifts so that the negative (balancing) feedback loop clearly dominates the system in the long term. In this section, we will explore the various types of common system behaviors to understand the feedback loops that drive them.

Figure 2.15 shows the same positive (reinforcing) feedback loop already covered earlier in this chapter and seen in Figures 2.1 and 2.3. It is an exponential growth curve. When the reader sees this type of behavior exhibited by a system, there must be a positive (reinforcing) feedback loop dominating the system (indicated by the circled + in the diagram). When analyzing the system, look for a set of elements that combine or connect together to create a vicious loop or virtuous loop.

Figure 2.16 will be an example used to discuss some of the following figures in this section. Figure 2.16 is a consequence map based on a project the author completed for the National Institutes of Health (NIH). An organization within NIH called the Center for Scientific Research (CSR) is the collection point for all the grant applications submitted to NIH. Of course, resources are required to review all these incoming applications to make decisions about which grants should be funded. The project focused on understanding how to forecast the resource requirements for this group. At this point, the entire consequence map in Figure 2.16 will

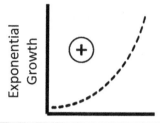

Figure 2.15   Positive (reinforcing) feedback loop.

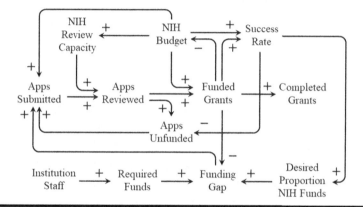

Figure 2.16   Consequence map for NIH grant applications.

not be discussed. The full consequence map is shown so the reader can see how multiple feedback loops are intertwined to make up a "system."

Figure 2.17 highlights a positive (reinforcing) feedback loop within the full consequence map for the NIH project. With no other interactions or disruptions, the feedback loop in Figure 2.17 would create the exponential growth behavior shown in Figure 2.15. This feedback loop describes a key management decision made by research organizations, and it starts with *Apps Submitted* (i.e., applications submitted) on the left side of the diagram. As a reminder, arrows show the direction of causality (i.e., cause and effect), and the + sign on the end of an arrow indicates that the two variables move in the same direction. That is, both variables increase, or both variables decrease. *Apps Submitted* leads to *Apps Reviewed*, which leads to *Funded Grants*. The more *Funded Grants* there are, the greater the *Success Rate*. For a research organization, the *Success Rate* affects how much funding the research organization will decide to seek from NIH. In Figure 2.17, a higher *Success Rate* leads to a higher *Desired Proportion NIH Funds*. In other words, the more success-ful the research organization is with obtaining NIH grants, the more the research organization will tend to seek NIH grants and move more resources toward chas-ing NIH grants. Compared to all other funding sources, the proportion of funds

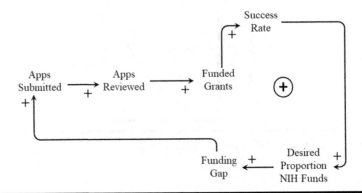

Figure 2.17   Positive (reinforcing) feedback loop for NIH grant applications.

sought from NIH would increase. In Figure 2.16, the *Funding Gap* is based on the level of staffing at the research organization compared to the amount of funding received (*Funded Grants*). The larger the staff, the more funding is required. The *Desired Proportion NIH Funds* drives this *Funding Gap*. Based on the magnitude of this *Funding Gap*, the research organization will submit more grant applications (*Apps Submitted*) in an effort to close the *Funding Gap*. This completes the feedback loop. If no other feedback loops interfered, this feedback loop would create growth for the research organization as more grant applications are submitted and funded, which encourages the research organization to submit even more grant applications to win more funding from NIH. Left alone, this feedback loop would exhibit the exponential growth behavior shown in Figure 2.15.

Figure 2.18 shows the same negative (balancing) feedback loop already covered earlier in this chapter and seen in Figures 2.6 and 2.7. Notice in Figure 2.18 that the "balancing" of the feedback loop can occur in either direction. In the earlier examples in Figures 2.6 and 2.7, the balancing mechanism works to take a "lower" value and bring it up to a "higher" value. This behavior is shown in the graph on the right of Figure 2.18. However, the left side of Figure 2.18 shows the opposite balancing behavior that works to take a "higher" value and bring it down to a "lower" value.

Figure 2.19 shows a negative (balancing) feedback loop in the NIH system. The *Funded Grants* are balanced by the *NIH Budget*. In essence, the NIH can only fund as many applications as the budget can accommodate. Left alone, this feedback

Goal-Seeking

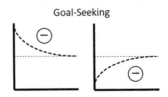

Figure 2.18   Negative (balancing) feedback loops.

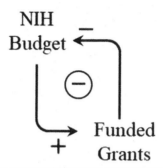

Figure 2.19 Negative (balancing) feedback loop for NIH grant applications.

loop would show the balancing behaviors in Figure 2.18. If the *NIH Budget* is high, the number of *Funded Grants* will increase to the level of the *NIH Budget* (like the right side of Figure 2.18). If the *NIH Budget* is low, the number of *Funded Grants* will decrease to the level of the *NIH Budget* (left side of Figure 2.18).

Figure 2.20 shows the combination of a positive (reinforcing) feedback loop and a negative (balancing) feedback loop interconnected to create an S-curve behavior. Figure 2.21 shows the combination of Figures 2.17 and 2.19 for the NIH grant application system. Left alone, the behavior generated by these two interconnected feedback loops would generate the behavior seen in Figure 2.20. In essence, there would be a growth in grant applications submitted up to the level of funding that can be supported by the *NIH Budget*. If the *NIH Budget* increases, over time more applications would be submitted. Conversely, if the *NIH Budget* decreases, over time less applications would be submitted. Of course, other elements impact all of this, but for the sake of simplicity at this point, if these were the only two feedback loops in operation the resulting behavior would be an S-curve.

The previous three behaviors (exponential curve, balancing curve, and S-curve) are a reiteration of the earlier sections, so the reader has seen them before.

S-Shaped

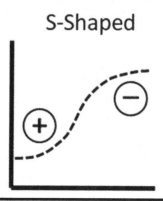

Figure 2.20 Typical S-curve.

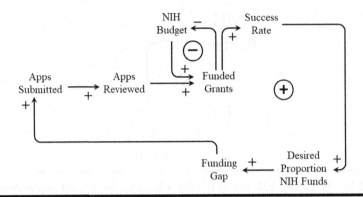

Figure 2.21 Combination of positive (reinforcing) and negative (balancing) feedback loops.

Figures 2.22 and 2.24 show different system behaviors. Figure 2.22 shows oscillatory behavior (i.e., repeating up and down). Oscillations are caused by a negative (balancing) feedback loop that has delays embedded in the system. Figure 2.23 shows the structure of this type of system.

As shown in the consequence map in Figure 2.23, this type of system has a *Delay* between the *Change in State* action and the *State of System* measurement. So, a change is made to the system (based on the magnitude of the *Gap*) to point the *State of System* toward the *Desired Goal*, but it takes a while for the system to experience the new change. As a result, the *State of System* continues to move in the same direction (because the change has not taken effect yet) and inadvertently goes past the *Desired Goal*. Then, when the *State of System* finally realizes the change and has a new value, the *State of System* is on the other side of the *Desired Goal* and now there is a *Gap* in the opposite direction, which creates a "whiplash" action as the *State of System* tries to turn around to get back to the *Desired Goal*. But, again, the *Delay* after the *Change in State* action causes the *State of System* to surpass the *Desired Goal* in the other direction, and so the whiplash reversal occurs again. Each time, the *Delay* causes the *State of System* to shoot past the *Desired Goal*.

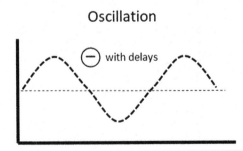

Figure 2.22 Oscillations due to negative (balancing) feedback loop with a delay.

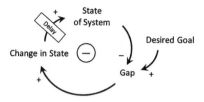

Figure 2.23 Oscillations due to negative (balancing) feedback loop with a delay.

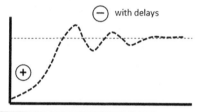

Figure 2.24 Typical S-curve followed with oscillations.

Consider the example of a metronome. The *Desired Goal* is for the arm to be straight up, which is the center point. When the metronome arm is moved, the system tries to balance itself back to the center resting point. But, the momentum of the arm causes it to go past the center point. For instance, if you pull the arm of a metronome to the left, it travels to the right and goes past the center point. Then, the arm slows down and heads left again toward the center. Once again, the arm passes through the center point and ends up on the left (which is where it started). Then, the arm turns around again and goes back to the right, and so on.

Figure 2.24 shows the combination of an S-curve (Figure 2.20) with oscillations (Figure 2.22). In this case, the system experiences growth in the beginning and then hits a limiting "balancing" factor with a negative feedback loop. However, the negative feedback loop has delays in it, so the transition to the new equilibrium point is not as smooth as shown in the traditional S-curve. Instead, there is a little bit of overshoot as the slow delay prevents the system from stopping smoothly at the new desired goal. Then, there is some oscillation as the system keeps going back and forth past the desired goal. The oscillations shrink over time so that eventually the oscillations go away and the system settles at the new desired goal.

A pendulum is a good example of the shrinking oscillations type of behavior. Like the metronome example from the previous paragraph, pulling the pendulum to the left of center causes the pendulum to oscillate around the center point. However, unlike the metronome, which has a counterbalance to keep the oscillations going indefinitely, the pendulum eventually slows down so that the back-and-forth oscillations get smaller, and finally stops with the pendulum back at rest in the center.

Another good example is taking a shower in an old building and trying to adjust the water temperature. In older buildings, the water is typically heated by a boiler in the basement of the building. If you are on a high floor, there is a long delay from the source of the hot water to your shower. When you get in the shower, the water is cold, so you frantically turn the faucet to make the water hotter. But, there is a delay, so the water remains cold. The typical reaction at that point is to turn the hot water further (because it has not responded yet). Thus, you "overcompensate." Then, when the hot water arrives, it is way too hot, so you have the frantically turn the faucet in the other direction to get cold water back. Again, there is a delay for the cold water to arrive, so the typical reaction is to turn the water even colder. Of course, when the cold water begins to arrive, it is way too cold. So, this back-and-forth behavior continues until the turns of the faucet are smaller and the desired temperature is finally found. Whew!

The behavior seen in Figure 2.24 is a more realistic example of what might be experienced in the real world given the two feedback loops in the NIH system shown in Figure 2.21. Notice the *Delay* on the right side of the consequence map between *Success Rate* and *Desired Proportion NIH Funds*. In an organization, it usually takes some time to realize that a situation has changed significantly (i.e., a state system variable has changed, such as *Success Rate*), and then it takes additional time to make a management decision based on the change because management wants to be sure that the change is not a temporary "blip." With this structure, if the *NIH Budget* increases, we might expect to see this behavior with the number of applications that get submitted to NIH.

For example, there was a 5-year time period when the *NIH Budget* actually doubled from 1998 to 2003. With the massive increase in available NIH funds, organizations tended to submit more grant applications to gain more funding. This makes complete sense. More funds are available, so go for it. At one point, NIH received as many grants in a single year as had previously taken 2.5 years. As more grants got funded (due to the higher *NIH Budget*), the *Success Rate* increased in the short term, which encouraged research organizations to seek more funding from NIH. In fact,

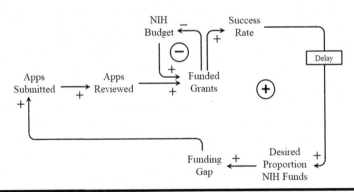

Figure 2.25 Negative (balancing) feedback loop with a delay.

some organizations went so far as to dedicate all resources to seeking grants only from NIH. This is exactly what happened at NIH. Applications greatly increased, and organizations began to rely on NIH funding. However, when the *NIH Budget* leveled out (i.e., no more increases), organizations were left with new facility expansions and new staff expansions that needed funding, so the organizations continued to bombard NIH with excessive grant applications. This is the overshoot part of the curve in Figure 2.23. The dynamics from this change are still ongoing. But, based on the structure of the feedback loops, we can expect oscillations to continue for years as organizations remove facilities and staff and rely on NIH less (which means less grant applications). After that change in capacity (assuming the *NIH Budget* doesn't change), less applications will be coming to NIH, which will result in more applications receiving funding because there is plenty of *NIH Budget* to go around (when compared to the lower amount of applications). This increases the *Success Rate*, which then pushes the oscillation in the opposite direction as research organizations make changes to increase their reliance on NIH funding again, and so on. Eventually, this system would settle down to an application rate that is commensurate with the *NIH Budget* and the "acceptable" or "expected" *Success Rate*.

The Kaibab Plateau

As another real-world example of the behavior shown in Figure 2.24, consider the Kaibab Plateau ecosystem. In the early 1900s, the deer herd population on the Kaibab Plateau on the north side of the Grand Canyon in Arizona was about 4000 (Figure 2.26). At that time, a bounty was placed on cougars, wolves, and coyotes, all of which were natural predators of deer. Within 15 to 20 years, there was a substantial reduction of these predators (from hunting) and a consequent and immediate spike in the deer population. During that time, the deer population had increased more than ten-fold. There was documented evidence by investigators of over-browsing of the area, which should have been a warning that there was a problem with the balance of the ecosystem. Yet, this did not produce a much-needed quick change in either the bounty policy or the potential removal of deer (to reduce the over-browsing of the vegetation). In the absence of predation by its natural predators or by man as the hunter, the deer herd reached a population of about 100,000 in the next few years. In the absence of sufficient food due to over-browsing, the majority of the herd died off in two successive winters. By then, the girdling of so much of the vegetation through over-browsing precluded recovery of the food reserve to such an extent that there was subsequent die-off and reduced birth rates. In the end, the deer herd population settled down at a level that was much less than the population that could theoretically have been maintained by the ecosystem.

A simulation model was constructed by Dr. John Sterman and others in the System Dynamics Group at the Massachusetts Institute of Technology (MIT)

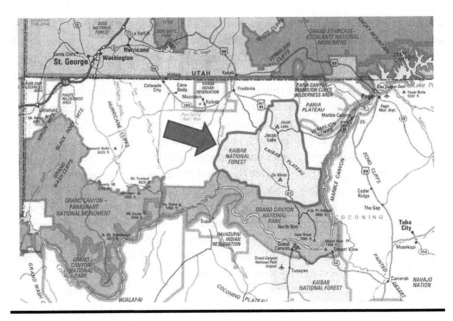

Figure 2.26   Kaibab Plateau.

Sloan School of Management to understand and analyze the Kaibab Plateau issue. Figure 2.27 shows the results of the baseline simulation that approximately replicated the results of historical data collected for the Kaibab Plateau. The solid black line (1) in the graph shows the *Deer Population*, the dashed dark gray line (2) shows the *Predator Population*, and the dotted light gray line (3) shows the *Food* (vegetation) available to the deer. As can be seen, the *Predator Population* is reduced to zero as a result of the hunting policy. The *Deer Population* then explodes quickly with no predators. During this spike in *Deer Population*, the *Food* is decreased significantly. After a period of massive starvation and die-off, the *Deer Population* and *Food* reach new (yet undesirable) equilibrium levels.

While the *Deer Population* line in Figure 2.27 does not exactly match Figure 2.24, the reader can see the rapid increase (positive feedback loop of the S-curve) that drives the *Deer Population* beyond the level that is sustainable by the *Food* source (negative feedback loop of the S-curve). Because it takes time for the *Food* to regenerate and grow back (delay in the negative feedback loop), the *Deer Population* first suffers a massive overshoot and then oscillates back and forth for a short time until the *Deer Population* finally settles at a level that is sustainable by the *Food*. Figure 2.28 shows the consequence map for the Kaibab Plateau example. The figure is a modification of the S-curve structure from Figure 2.11.

As stated earlier in this chapter, not all systems exhibit behavior that is easily identifiable with one of the types of behavior curves shown in this chapter. However, in a general sense, anytime the changes that occur over each time period tend to increase, a positive (reinforcing) feedback loop is most likely driving the

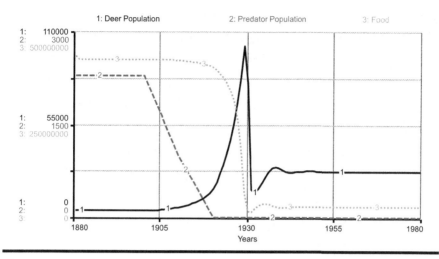

Figure 2.27 Behavior of Kaibab Plateau key variables.

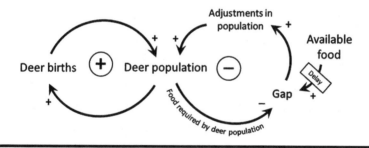

Figure 2.28 S-curve feedback loop structure for Kaibab Plateau.

system. Conversely, anytime the changes that occur over each time period tend to shrink, a negative (balancing) feedback loop is mostly driving the system. And, when there are oscillations, the reader can be sure that a negative (balancing) feedback loop with significant delays is driving the system.

So Why Does This Matter?

In the complex systems that we typically operate within (e.g., companies, organizations, major societal issues), feedback loops are the fundamental building blocks of the system structure. As discussed in this chapter, fortunately there are only two types of feedback loops: positive (reinforcing) feedback loops that drive change in the *same* direction as the initial change, and negative (balancing) feedback loops that drive change in the *opposite* direction of the initial change. However, when multiple feedback loops interconnect and share some of the same elements, the behaviors of these systems tend to be counterintuitive. In other words, our typical "thinking" (i.e., our intuition) is opposite of what the behavior truly is. We want to push on Element XYZ in the system, but really the better solution is to push on Element ABC. Or, we want to push Element XYZ in one direction, but really the better solution is to push Element XYZ in the opposite direction.

As discussed in Chapter 1, our minds tend to see the world as simple, linear cause-and-effect chains. Or, if we think about a feedback loop at all, we assume the feedback loop has no delays and is very quick to react. However, as shown in this chapter, feedback loops can contain delays between one element (cause) and another element (effect). These delays can be very large so that they happen over a very long time period (i.e., weeks, months, or years). For this, we say that the cause and effect are separated by *time*. In complex systems, the cause and effect within a feedback loop can also be separated by *space*, which means that the cause (which happens in one part of the system) results in an effect that is experienced somewhere else in the system "far away" from the cause. For example, in an organization, a policy change in the finance department (e.g., capturing employee hours every day instead of every week) may result in an effect that is experienced in the human resources department (e.g., many people forget to turn in their time sheets daily because they are used to the weekly pace, so exceptions have to be made frequently, which takes a lot of extra time). The cause (policy change) and effect (extra time fixing time sheets) are widely separated in the system.

In talking about the separation of cause and effect within a feedback loop in both time and space, the term *tight* is used to refer to a feedback loop in which cause and effect have no delays and occur very close to each other so that the effect is quickly experienced. The term *loose* is used to refer to a feedback loop in which cause and effect are separated by significant time delays and the effect is experienced somewhere within the system far away from the original cause. In the real world, complex systems are a combination of many interconnected feedback loops of various degrees of tightness or looseness. Thus, an element within one feedback loop that is tight may also be in a feedback loop that is loose such that the tighter feedback loop reacts first, and the looser feedback loops happens over a much longer period of time. Sometimes, that delay is enough to make people "forget" about the initial system change that kicked off the loose feedback loop. Instead, people just remember the "quick" consequence shown by the tight feedback loop. This is why short-term behavior and long-term behavior within a system can be vastly different. The difference in behavior is caused by the tight and loose feedback loops. As shown by the S-curve, the tighter positive feedback loop is eventually overcome by the looser negative feedback loop. These changes in tight and loose feedback loops cause one loop to dominate the system over one period of time and another feedback loop to dominate the system over another period of time. This is called a shift in loop dominance.

Here is a quick summary of the key concerns for complex systems:

- Feedback loops (the structure of complex systems) in larger systems tend to have longer delays and tend to be spread out over wider areas of the overall system. In many cases, it is extremely difficult even to see the entirety of some of the feedback loops because they are so far-reaching.
- Multiple feedback loops interconnect so that a single action taken for a single element within a single feedback loop can have multiple, simultaneous "ripple effects" in other feedback loops that reach out to other parts of the overall system.
- The impact from one element (cause) to another element (effect) within a feedback loop is often non-linear. This means that changes are not always proportional to the action taken. So, if the action is X and the result is Y, this means that 2X does not always produce 2Y. Sometimes, 2X may only produce 1.5Y. Or, 2X may produce 5Y. This non-linearity makes it difficult to "calibrate" our actions because the result can sometimes be much smaller or much larger than expected. Similar to the example of adjusting the hot water in an old building, when delays are added to the system, one action taken can continue to amplify the results beyond what we intended due to the non-linearity.

All of these previous bullet points create situations in which unintended consequences occur because other parts of the system (other than our own part of the system) are impacted in ways that we typically do not know when making out initial action. We may successfully achieve our intended consequences, but there will almost always be unintended consequences and, if significant enough, these unintended consequences can even overcome or overpower our initial success. Our minds want the world to be single, linear cause-and-effect chains. Yet, the world is really a hodge-podge of multiple, non-linear feedback loops of varying strength and time scales. No wonder we struggle with issues like poverty, racism, and the like. Getting all the elements together on a single consequence map for tracing feedback loops proves very time-consuming and difficult, so we skip it and just apply myopic policies that may work in the short term but have worse consequences in the long term.

Is the reader starting to feel hopeless with the complexity embodied in multiple, non-linear feedback systems? If so, Chapter 3 on consequence maps will begin to reveal an approach that can used to tackle these unwieldy systems.

Bibliography

Forrester, Jay W., *Industrial Dynamics*, Cambridge, MA: Productivity Press, 1961.
Forrester, Jay W., *Collected Papers of Jay W. Forrester*, Cambridge, MA: Wright-Allen Press, 1975.
Sterman, J. D., *Business Dynamics: Systems Thinking and Modeling for a Complex World*, New York: Irwin/McGraw-Hill, 2000.
White, J. Chris and Sholtes, Robert M., *The Dynamic Progress Method: Using Advanced Simulation to Improve Project Planning and Management*, Boca Raton, FL: CRC Press, 2016.

CONSEQUENCE MAPS

2

Chapter 3

Creating Consequence Maps

Chapters 1 and 2 hopefully provided enough motivation for why the consequence map is a powerful tool for strategic planning, analyzing complex issues, balancing tradeoffs, and understanding how systems can show beneficial results in the short term but detrimental results in the long term (or vice versa). This chapter will focus specifically on how to create and draw consequence maps. The steps are fairly simple in nature, but that does not mean that it is a simple approach. Creating useful and realistic consequence maps takes quite a bit of practice.

Team-Based Development

When it comes to consequence maps, two heads are definitely better than one. And, three heads are better than two. The more, the merrier (up to a point, of course). The objective of a consequence map is to capture the desired "system" in its entirety. Rarely does any one single person have this wide-reaching perspective. No person has all the answers. And, if the person did have the full perspective, that person would still have biases that limit the effectiveness of the consequence map. As a result, it is best to use a team of several people involved with the system or issue from multiple perspectives. Each person will have details and perspectives not shared by others. And, where there is overlap, that overlap just helps increase the confidence that the consequence map is capturing elements and relationships correctly. Imagine that each person's view of the system is like a puzzle piece. It takes several people with several puzzle pieces to put together the entire puzzle.

Nouns and Relationships

The first thing to know about consequence maps is that every element in the map should be a "noun." We want elements that go up and down in value (i.e., increase or decrease in value), which means that we want "things" (which are nouns). A short example demonstrates this. Figure 3.1 shows two ways to present the same concept: having more money makes someone feel better. Of course, the reader may not agree with this statement, but for the sake of the example, this will be the premise.

The top part of Figure 3.1 is the typical way one might say this: When I get more money, I feel better. In this case, getting more money leads to feeling better. So, it would be easy to draw a cause-and-effect relationship between *Get more money* and *Feel better*, as shown in the top part of Figure 3.1. Essentially, we are saying that getting more money causes the effect of feeling better. And, this cause-and-effect relationship would be correct. There is nothing "wrong" with this drawing. However, it is very limiting. What if I had less money? How is that represented? Using this approach, another cause-and-effect relationship would need to be drawn between "having less money" and "feeling worse."

Instead, a better method would be to represent both the cause and effect as nouns that represent "quantities" that can go up and down (i.e., increase and decrease). If done this way, the relationship will hold for both "getting more money makes me feel better" and "having less money makes me feel worse." The bottom part of Figure 3.1 shows this method. The cause-and-effect relationship at the bottom of Figure 3.1 states that the *Amount of money* I have (which is a quantity that can go up and down) impacts the *Amount of positive feeling* I have (which is also a quantity that can go up and down). To compare the two methods, "having more money" corresponds to a high value for the *Amount of money* I have. Conversely, "having less money" corresponds to a low value for the *Amount of money* I have. In the same way, "feeling better" corresponds to a high value for the *Amount of positive feeling* I have. And, "feeling worse" corresponds to a low value for the *Amount of positive feeling* I have. Using nouns that represent quantities that can go up and down (increase and decrease) offers a much more appropriate method for representing the relationship.

After making the elements nouns that can increase and decrease in quantity, the next step is to establish the correct causal relationship between the two elements. Fortunately, there are only two choices. Suppose there is a cause that increases in

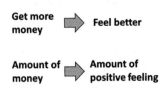

Figure 3.1 Using nouns for elements.

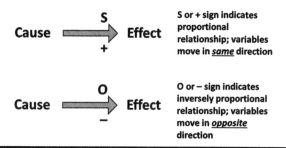

Figure 3.2   Types of cause-and-effect relationships.

value (e.g., we get more money). The resulting effect can only go in one of two directions. The effect can either increase (similar to the cause) or the effect can decrease (opposite of the cause). If the effect moves in the same direction (e.g., more money causes more positive feeling), the relationship is categorized as *proportional*. The two move in the same direction. In this case, either an S or a + sign is put at the head of the arrow that indicates the direction of causality (top part of Figure 3.2).

On the other hand, if the effect moves in the opposite direction (e.g., more sunlight causes less moisture on the ground), the relationship is categorized as *inversely proportional*. The two move in opposite directions. In this case, either an O or a – sign is put at the head of the arrow that indicates the direction of causality (bottom part of Figure 3.2).

Putting Figures 3.1 and 3.2 together, we get Figure 3.3. There is a proportional relationship between the cause (*Amount of money*) and the resulting effect (*Amount of positive feeling*). Hence, an S is placed at the arrowhead (as in the top of Figure 3.3), or a + sign is put at the arrowhead (as in the bottom part of Figure 3.3). Both of these mean the same thing. As a consequence map is constructed, make sure to maintain consistency. Either use only Ss and Os, or use only + and – signs.

To summarize to this point, use nouns for the elements in the consequence map. These are values that can go up and down (i.e., increase and decrease in value). Use an arrow to indicate the direction of causality (i.e., cause and effect), with a sign at the head of the arrow to indicate whether the elements move in the same direction (proportional relationship, S or +) or the elements move in opposite directions (inversely proportional relationship, O or –).

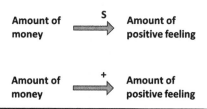

Figure 3.3   Figure 3.1 redrawn with correct relationship.

Believe it or not, that is the basic approach for the mechanics of creating consequence maps. The following sections will provide some suggestions and methods that are helpful and enable the reader to increase his or her effectiveness for drawing the maps.

Laundry Lists and Circles

When first creating consequence maps, it can be difficult to draw cause-and-effect relationships immediately. A useful approach at this point is to create a "laundry list" of elements that need to be included, even if the cause-and-effect relationships are not known yet. For instance, suppose we wanted to create a simple consequence map for the cycle of poverty. Of course, a full consequence map would be very extensive, so this map does not at all attempt to diagram the issue of poverty completely. But, as a simple example of the approach, we might start with a list of elements we know we want to include in the consequence map. This list might be obtained through some brainstorming exercise or simply by letting each person on the development team suggest some elements that they know play a part in the system or issue. In this example, the following is the list of elements that we want to make sure are in our consequence map in some form or another:

- Poverty
- Reduced physical, mental, or work capacities
- Infectious diseases
- Malnutrition
- Reduced economic impact

This is our "laundry list." We now have a starting point. As we continue to build the consequence map with the team, other elements may be added to make the list longer, but as a starting point let us suppose that these are the key elements we see playing a role in the cycle of poverty. The next step would be to lay out these elements and begin to draw cause-and-effect connections between and among the elements. A common approach is to put all the elements from the laundry list in a circle so that it is easy to draw a connection from any element to any other element (Figures 3.4 and 3.5). Sometimes the connection arrows will overlap each other as they criss-cross throughout the circle. That is okay. This is just a first step and is a simple way to get the most information about the system. As will be shown in the following paragraphs of this section of this chapter, as well as Chapters 4 through 6, the circle will be cleaned up once all the connections are known.

Notice in Figure 3.5 that some of the elements do not follow the noun rule for elements. At this point, that is fine. At these beginning stages, it is sometimes helpful to let people on the team describe the elements in their own words. Do not stifle the team process. Just make sure the intent of the element is fully understood. It will be a huge stepping stone just to have all this in a single view. In most cases, this

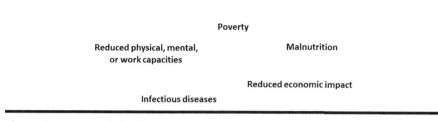

Figure 3.4   Lay out the elements in the laundry list.

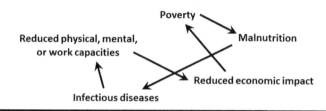

Figure 3.5   Causal connections between the elements.

type of mapping will have never occurred yet. The consequence mapping exercise will be the first time to draw the complete picture, so do not worry about nitpicking yet.

Cause-and-Effect Connections

Eventually, we do want the map cleaned up and drawn properly. So, the next step would be to make the elements nouns (that go up and down) and clarify the types of relationships between the elements already connected in Figure 3.5. Figure 3.6 shows a final map for this simple example. Starting at the top of Figure 3.6, the *Level of poverty* has an opposite effect on the *Level of nutrition*. The more impoverished a person is, generally, the lower the nutrition level is for that person because the person cannot afford to buy healthier foods and supplements, which cost more money. The *Level of nutrition* has an opposite effect on the *Amount of infectious diseases* for the person. In other words, the better the nutrition level for the person, the less diseases or sickness the person will typically suffer. The *Amount of infectious diseases* then has an opposite impact on the *Level of physical, mental, or work capacities*. That is, the sicker a person is, the less capable the person for doing useful work due to physical or mental limitations. Next, the *Level of physical, mental, or work capacities* causes an impact in the same direction for the *Amount of economic impact*. A person with high physical or mental abilities will generally be able to find a well-paying job. The fewer employable skills a person has, typically the less wages that person can earn. Finally, the *Amount of economic impact* has an opposite effect

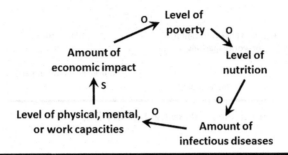

Figure 3.6 Completed consequence map.

on the *Level of poverty*. That is, the more gainfully employed a person is, the better chance the person stands of being less impoverished, because they are being paid a good salary or wages.

Identify Feedback Loops

After drawing a consequence map like the one in Figure 3.6, it is time to highlight the feedback loops in the map because the feedback loops are the structures that will drive the behavior of the system. In this simple example, Figure 3.6 shows only one feedback loop. A feedback loop occurs when the arrows of causality start at one element, travel around through other elements, and come back to impact the original element. Remember, there are only two types of feedback loops: positive (reinforcing) feedback loops and negative (balancing) feedback loops. The method for determining the polarity of the feedback loop is to count the Os or − signs. If the number of Os or − signs is even, the feedback loop is a positive, reinforcing feedback loop. If the number of Os or − signs is odd, the feedback loop is a negative, balancing feedback loop. Figure 3.7 shows the calculation for the consequence map from Figure 3.6. We start by pretending that one of the elements (*Level of poverty*) increases (thick black arrow labeled with the number 1). Then, we follow the ups and downs around the loop and see what the final impact on that same element (*Level of poverty*) is. Keep in mind, the thick black arrows will switch directions when an O (opposite) is encountered. So, if the *Level of poverty* increases (thick black arrow labeled with the number 1), the *Level of nutrition* decreases (thick black arrow labeled with the number 2), which causes the *Amount of infectious diseases* to increase (thick black arrow labeled with the number 3), and so on. In the end, with the thick gray arrow labeled with the number 6, the loop goes full circle to drive the *Level of poverty* in the same direction with which we started (i.e., an increase). By tracing the up/down arrows, we see that this is a positive, reinforcing feedback loop since the net effect is to move the original element in the *same* direction. (It would be a negative, balancing feedback loop if the net effect is to move the original element in the *opposite*

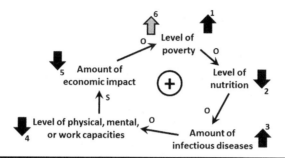

Figure 3.7 Positive (reinforcing) feedback loop.

direction.) Yet, a simpler approach is to count the Os. There are four (4) Os, which is an even number and indicates the positive, reinforcing feedback loop. Essentially, every pair of two Os cancel each other out.

In Figure 3.7, the element *Level of poverty* may sound a little strange. In Figure 3.8, the element *Level of poverty* has been changed to *Level of wealth* because that is a more common way of expressing the sentiment. Notice that when *Level of poverty* is changed to *Level of wealth*, the causal relationships change, also. The *Level of wealth* now has a proportional (same) relationship to the *Level of nutrition*: the more money someone has, the higher that person's level of nutrition. In Figure 3.7, the causal relationship between *Level of poverty* and *Level of nutrition* was inversely proportional (opposite). In Figure 3.8, the causal relationship between *Amount of economic impact* and *Level of wealth* has also changed. Now, the *Amount of economic impact* has a proportional (same) relationship to the *Level of wealth*: the higher amount of economic impact, typically the higher the level of wealth. An interesting thing about consequence maps is that, depending on how the variables are defined, the cause-and-effect relationships between the elements can change, yet, notice that Figure 3.8 still shows a positive, reinforcing feedback loop (even number of Os).

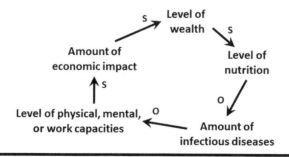

Figure 3.8 Positive (reinforcing) feedback loop, even with different elements.

What Happens Next?

The previous sections in the chapter discuss the key activities for creating consequence maps. This section and the following section will provide a couple of techniques that help the facilitator of the consequence map development sessions.

The simple poverty cycle example makes it look fairly easy to draw consequence maps. This is not the case. It takes time and practice. For example, the laundry list and resulting consequence map in Figures 3.7 and 3.8 are quite insufficient. Many more elements could easily be added. As the facilitator of consequence mapping sessions, for any and all elements it is important to always ask members of the team "What happens next?" or "What does this impact?" This forces team members to look beyond just a few elements. While it could be argued that a chain of cause-and-effect linkages could be infinite, obviously, a line in the sand needs to be drawn. The objective is to strike the appropriate balance between having enough elements in the map to cover the scope of the system or issue, but not so many elements that it unnecessarily adds complexity to the map beyond what is needed. This balance is often difficult to find. When drawing consequence maps for the first few times, it is easy (and natural) to fall back on a very limited list of elements. Thus, asking everyone, "What happens next?" or "What does this impact?" takes the group beyond this limited list. As you facilitate more consequence map development sessions, you will begin to get a better feel for when enough elements are in the map and when more elements need to be added to meet the scope of the problem or issue.

Close the Loops

In the poverty cycle example, a feedback loop already existed. However, when working with a team to develop a consequence map, feedback loops will not always appear right away. An impact of the "What happens next?" line of questioning is that it extends the cause-and-effect chains to make longer chains. Imagine starting at one point on the globe and walking in a straight line. After a very long walk (assuming there was always land in your pathway), you would eventually come back around to your starting point. That is the same with cause-and-effect chains. Eventually, the chain will become long enough that it wraps around to itself again. In other words, the original element that started as a cause will eventually become the effect of some other cause in the chain. Without asking "What happens next?" the cause-and-effect chains would tend to be very short and straight and would not provide feedback loops. However, feedback loops are the key structures that drive the behavior of systems, so as a facilitator you need to help the team find them. As a result, if your team has drawn a consequence map that consists of several straight-line cause-and-effect chains that have a single starting point and a different ending point, your work is not complete. Every system or issue contains at least one feedback loop. Continue to work with the team until one or more cause-and-effect chains closes back onto itself to make a feedback loop.

Because systems often share similar structures (i.e., similar feedback loops), this task will become easier as you develop more consequence maps. For example, in one system consequence map the team may have identified a balancing feedback loop that balances company expenditures with available funds. That is, if expenditures are high but available funds are low, there will be financial control mechanisms in the company to reduce expenditures (because there is not much money available). This feedback loop is common to all organizations. Thus, when you are facilitating another consequence map workshop with another team, if the system or issue being analyzed involves the organization, you can feel pretty confident that this financial control loop will (or should) appear somewhere in the consequence map.

Use Lots of Space

A final point to make for facilitating consequence map development sessions is to give ample space for drawing. There will be many changes to the consequence map as the session progresses and each participant adds their knowledge to the diagram, and then each participant changes their inputs based on newly revealed elements and relationships in the ongoing development of the map. There will be many iterations of the map. The first iteration may just be the laundry list. The next iteration may be the circle of elements with lines drawn among them. Another iteration may be an attempt to clean up the diagram to remove as many criss-crossing lines as possible. And so on, and so on.

This ample space can be accomplished with multiple whiteboards or large sheets of paper. My favorite approach is to use a large roll of butcher paper because then I can cover an entire wall, if needed, based on the size and scope of the issue, problem, or system at hand.

Never be afraid to start over with regard to drawing. The main objective is to get the elements and relationships correct. Making the diagram look nice is secondary.

Real-World Example: Asset Management for a City Water Delivery System

This section looks at an example from a magazine article and walks through the development of the consequence map for the issue discussed. This example was used with a water services department for a city in Texas that was struggling with the exact issue highlighted in the article. All iterations of output from the group will not be discussed to keep this section short. However, enough will be shown to allow the reader to see the steps involved, the discussions that occurred, and the resulting consequence map.

The article was "Conveyance Catch-22" in *Water Efficiency* magazine (author Carol Brzozowski, November/December 2010 issue). The article was about the aging of the assets and infrastructure of many municipal water delivery systems (i.e., conveyance systems). It provided several examples, such as an 8-inch cast-iron water main break in Dallas in 2010 that flooded lower levels of a municipal building and killed the building's electrical system. As another example, within one month in 2009, 43 water main breaks occurred in Los Angeles, which flooded many business buildings and excessively blocked traffic. One pipe was 90 years old. The article went on to describe the nation-wide aging infrastructure in the U.S. (with water conveyance systems included) and the lack of funding to fix or replace this infrastructure, an estimated cost of $2.2 trillion. Consequently, many cities are in a reactive maintenance mode, instead of predictive or preventative maintenance. The Catch-22 is that many municipalities struggle to find the money to make improvements now in the short term, but ignoring the aging assets and aging infrastructure problems only makes them worse in the long run, with larger financial implications in the future. This has often been called the "maintenance death spiral" because the problem just keeps getting worse and worse.

The team for this effort was composed of seven people: the manager of the water department, two maintenance personnel from the water department, a financial analyst with the city, a city engineer, a person from the public works department, and myself. This represented a good mix of people that all could see part of the system or issue, but not the entire system or issue.

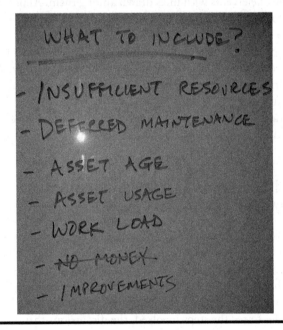

Figure 3.9 Laundry list of elements for asset management death spiral.

We started with a laundry list of system elements that might play a role the maintenance death spiral, as shown in Figure 3.9. This was done by going around the group and asking them to add to a list on the whiteboard. Notice that the list in Figure 3.9 is not that long. Often, at this point in the process, everyone is very focused on a specific issue and may not be able to see or consider elements from a "broader" system view. That is fine. The point is to get a list started and to get some level of agreement and consensus on the list.

Once the laundry list was created as a starting point (and there were other iterations of this list as the effort continued), we tried to connect some of the elements to establish causal relationships. Figure 3.10 shows a portion of these relationships. Again, the focus was on understanding the maintenance death spiral, so it is clear in Figure 3.10 that the focus was limited because there were only a few elements in the diagram. In Figure 3.10, we started with *Insufficient Resources* (the first element in the laundry list from Figure 3.9). The question was asked by me, "If there are not enough people to do the maintenance work, what happens?" The response from the team was, "If we don't have people to do the work (due to lack of budget), no work gets done. We delay the work until we have people that can do the work." Thus, *Insufficient Resources* leads to *Maintenance Deferrals*.

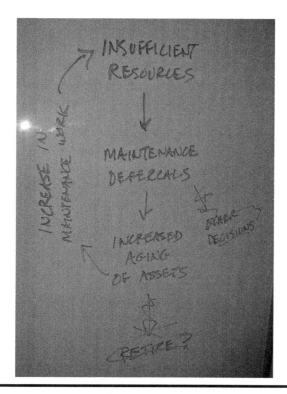

Figure 3.10   First draft of feedback loop for death spiral.

The rest of the conversation went as follows:

Me: "If maintenance can't be done for the assets, what happens to the assets?"

Team: "The assets stay in service and we just keep using them, which means they get more worn out with wear and tear. They essentially get older because they eat up their remaining service life. Giving them a break and doing maintenance keeps them from getting old too fast. It helps them last longer."

[Thus, in Figure 3.10, Maintenance Deferrals causes Increased Aging of Assets.]

Me: "Why does that matter? So they get a little older. Is that a big deal?"

Team: "Well, as the assets get older, they tend to require more maintenance work. It gets more difficult to do the same work because of dirt, corrosion, or things like that. For a brand new piece of equipment, the maintenance work might be very minimal. But, over time, those same maintenance tasks take longer and longer. And, they typically happen more frequently. So, instead of doing maintenance once a year, we're doing maintenance twice a year or three times a year."

[Thus, in Figure 3.10, Increased Aging of Assets leads to an Increase in Maintenance Work.]

Me: "Ok, so you have more maintenance work to do. The older the assets, the more maintenance work. Got it. Is there a problem with having more maintenance work?"

Team: "Of course! We started off saying we didn't have enough resources to do the regular work that needed to be done. Now, we have even more work to do on top of the regular work. But, we still don't have enough resources. It snowballs and makes the situation worse. Aha! We have a feedback loop!"

[Thus, in Figure 3.10, the Increase in Maintenance Work leads back to Insufficient Resources to complete the feedback loop.]

At that point in the effort, the team felt pretty good about drawing a feedback loop that captured the maintenance death spiral: *Insufficient Resources* leads to *Maintenance Deferrals*, which causes *Increased Aging of Assets* and results in an *Increase in Maintenance Work*, which ultimately comes back around again to highlight the *Insufficient Resources*.

While this did, indeed, capture the death spiral feedback loop at a high level, it was not enough to do take action. We needed more elements of the underlying system. This resulted in several discussions and new laundry lists of elements to

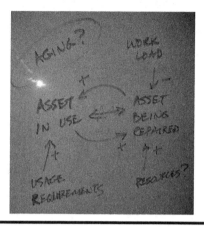

Figure 3.11   Additional elements for asset management.

include. Figure 3.11 shows the results of one of these discussions. This discussion focused on the "path of the asset" (as one team member called it). Either an asset is in service and being used, or the asset is "offline" to get worked on (i.e., maintenance). Thus, the asset itself cycles between *Asset in Use* and *Asset Being Repaired*. Notice in the middle of the diagram is a two-headed arrow. This is how the relationship was first drawn. We then clarified the relationships to show that items being used (i.e., *Assets in Use*) get pulled out of service to go into maintenance (i.e., *Asset Being Repaired*). And, once the maintenance work is finished, the asset moves from being out of service (i.e., *Asset Being Repaired*) back into active service (i.e., *Asset in Use*). Now that we had an element called *Asset Being Repaired*, we could begin to look at the elements that impacted this. Consequently, the team made the connection between the maintenance *Work Load* and *Asset Being Repaired*: the more work there was, the fewer assets got moved back into service. Notice the – sign at the head of the arrow from *Work Load* to *Asset Being Repaired* indicating this inversely proportional (opposite) causal relationship. Furthermore, the team made the connection between the *Resources* available for maintenance work and *Asset Being Repaired*: the more resources that were available, the more assets got moved back into service. Notice the + sign at the head of the arrow from *Resources* to *Asset Being Repaired* indicating this proportional (same) causal relationship.

The team continued to work through other elements in the system to expand the consequence map. After several iterations, we settled on the consequence map shown in Figure 3.12. Starting in the upper left of Figure 3.12, the reader sees the refinement of the "path of the asset." Assets begin in *Available Assets* (i.e., assets in service and available for use). These are *Removed from Service* periodically for maintenance work, to become *Unavailable Assets* (i.e., assets in the repair shop). This is accomplished either by physically bringing the asset in to the maintenance shop or by taking the asset offline and conducting the maintenance work at the location of the asset. After these assets are repaired, they are

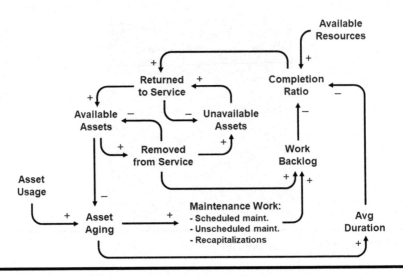

Figure 3.12 Final consequence map for asset management.

Returned to Service and are available to be used again. The arrows with − signs indicate that the more assets that are *Removed from Service*, the less *Available Assets* there are for service. And, the more assets that are *Returned to Service*, the less *Unavailable Assets* there are in repair.

As assets are *Removed from Service*, there is an increase in the *Work Backlog* (i.e., maintenance work load), which is also based on the amount of *Maintenance Work* for the asset. Notice that maintenance work actually includes multiple types of work: schedule maintenance work (i.e., monthly inspections), unscheduled maintenance work (i.e., unexpected breakdowns, failures), and recapitalizations (i.e., upgrades, service life extensions, work that lengthens the life of the asset). The measure for maintenance work getting accomplished is the *Completion Ratio*, which is the ratio of the *Available Resources* versus the *Work Backlog*. If the *Completion Ratio* is large, it means that there are more than sufficient *Available Resources* to do the work (+ arrow from *Available Resources* to *Completion Ratio*). Conversely, if the *Completion Ratio* is small, it means that the *Work Backlog* is more than the *Available Resources* can handle (i.e., insufficient resources) (− arrow from *Work Backlog* to *Completion Ratio*).

Going back to the lower left of Figure 3.12, *Asset Usage* represents the total "work" that the "fleet" of assets is supposed to do (e.g., pump water, store water). A high value for *Asset Usage* means that there is a lot of work that the assets need to do, and a low value for *Asset Usage* means that there is very little work that the assets need to do. Notice that *Asset Usage* has a direct impact on *Asset Aging*. The more the assets are used (e.g., the more hours of pumping water), the more they age. For example, a pump may have an expected service life of 5000 hours. If the asset is being used a lot (e.g., 500 hours per month), then the asset will age quickly and move through its service life quickly (e.g., the asset will last only 10 months, or less than 1 year). However, if the asset is used less frequently (e.g., 100 hours per month), then the asset will age slowly and move through its service life slowly (e.g., the asset will last 50 months, or more than 4 years).

Asset Aging then impacts the level of *Maintenance Work*. The higher the age of the asset (i.e., further along in its service life), the higher the *Maintenance Work* associated with the asset (+ arrow from *Asset Aging* to *Maintenance Work*), which, of course, increases the *Work Backlog*. *Asset Aging* also impacts how long it takes to do the work, so there is a + arrow from *Asset Aging* to *Avg Duration* (average duration of the service work) in the lower right corner of Figure 3.12. Similar to the opposite impact that *Work Backlog* has on the *Completion Ratio*, the *Avg Duration* also has an opposite impact on the *Completion Ratio*. The longer it takes to do the maintenance work, the less maintenance work gets accomplished.

With all the cause-and-effect relationships established, we can now trace through the consequence map to see the system elements that lead to the maintenance death spiral. Following the order of Figure 3.10, start in the upper right of Figure 3.13 with the gray highlighted element *Completion Ratio*. When there are insufficient *Available Resources*, the *Completion Ratio* decreases. When the *Completion Ratio* decreases, the number of assets *Returned to Service* also decreases, which leads to fewer *Available Assets*. When there are fewer *Available Assets* and the required *Asset Usage* stays constant, each asset that is available suffers more *Asset Aging* as each asset takes on more and more work (because there are fewer assets to spread the same amount of work around). The increase in *Asset Aging* leads to an increase in *Maintenance Work*. Assuming no change in the *Available Resources*, the *Completion*

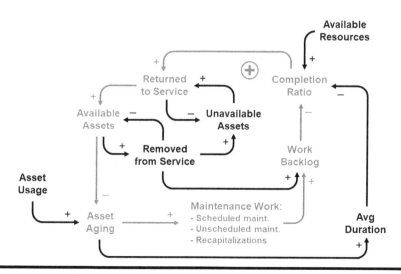

Figure 3.13 Positive (reinforcing) feedback loop for death spiral.

Ratio decreases even more, which completes the positive (reinforcing) feedback loop of the maintenance death spiral (highlighted in gray in Figure 3.13).

The team was quite surprised to see the full view of the system elements that drove the maintenance death spiral. It became very apparent how the department could get in the situation it was in with absolutely no "wrong-doing" or "sabotage" from anyone or any department in the city. It was clear that everyone could have the best intentions, yet the system could still suffer from the death spiral dynamics. The "politics" of the situation quickly fell away, and the discussion turned to solving the problem now that it was obvious how the problem manifested itself. Figure 3.14 shows two of the intervention points discussed by the team. The first and most obvious intervention in the system was to increase the *Available Resources* (the labor and material available to accomplish the maintenance work). As obvious as it was, this could not be the only solution to the problem, because this city did not have enough in its personnel budget to correct the problem. Based on the information at the time, the desired maintenance workforce would need to be about 75% higher than the current workforce. This magnitude of increase would never get approved by the city council. However, it was believed that a 25% to 30% increase might be approved.

The second option was to buy new assets and/or retire the old assets. Both of these would make the group of assets seem "newer" and the group of assets would, on average, have a longer service life. Based on the information at the time, about 40% of the assets would need to be retired and replaced with new assets to get to the desired "average age" for the fleet of assets. Similar to the workforce, this number seemed to be beyond anything the city council would approve. However, through a partnership with another nearby city that was willing to share assets

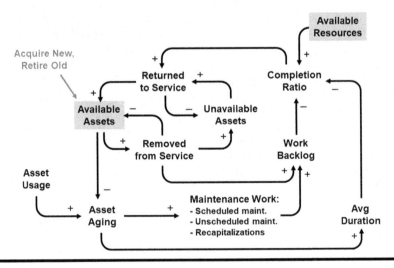

Figure 3.14   Intervention points to avoid death spiral.

along with the replacement of some of the city's current oldest assets, a net change of about 15% could be achieved. These two actions combined provided a large amount of relief for the city. The problem was not completely eliminated, but there was a definite improvement.

As a third option (not highlighted in Figure 3.14), the city implemented a Lean Six Sigma project that improved the efficiency and productivity of the maintenance workforce, which increased the maintenance workforce's capacity to do more maintenance work in the same amount of time. All of these changes took approximately 3 months to implement. In the end, due to other upcoming Lean Six Sigma projects, the city estimated that it would take only 6–9 more months for the system to correct itself fully to the point where there were sufficient resources to address all water system maintenance needs. At publication time for this book, the city was still on the path to gaining that level of equilibrium in the desired timeframe.

A Final Comment

Consequence maps are powerful tools for providing insight into very complex issues and problems, as well as de-politicizing the issues and problems to point to multiple options for interventions and corrections. A measure of the utility and effectiveness of a consequence map is its ability to transfer to other situations. A good consequence map transfers well to other systems. The consequence map in Figure 3.12 was shared with several defense organizations (both government and commercial) to see if the same dynamics held for military assets. Indeed, the dynamics of the problem are shared. Military assets and fleets (e.g., tanks, aircraft, ships, trucks, engines) suffer the exact same maintenance death spiral (although it may go by a slightly different name) as the water delivery systems for cities and municipalities. Moreover, the possible interventions are also shared. When the systems share the same consequence map for the same problem, the solution(s) to the problem in one system can also be transferred to the other systems. In Chapters 4, 5, and 6, the reader will see other example consequence maps and will most likely be able to sympathize with at least one of them.

Bibliography

Brzozowski, Carol, "Conveyance Catch-22," *Water Efficiency*, November/December 2010.

Chapter 4

Example Consequence Map for a City for a Major Change Initiative

This chapter walks through the specific use of consequence mapping to understand the short-term and long-term consequences of how a city (or any organization) should approach a major change initiative. In this case, the change initiative is the introduction and implementation of Lean Six Sigma (process improvement methodology) in a medium-sized city. However, the consequence map shown in this chapter can be generically applied for any type of major change within an organization by changing *Citizens* to *Customers*.

The Feedback Loops

The next several figures will each focus on one of the feedback loops found in the consequence map. The full, final consequence map is shown later in Figure 4.11. Of course, the consequence map was not created by developing each feedback loop independently (as it may appear with the figures). The consequence map was developed using the approach outlined in Chapter 3.

Figure 4.1 shows the balancing feedback loop due to citizen satisfaction. We will start with *Citizens*. The more *Citizens* that live in the city, the larger the backlog of work for the city employees (e.g., checking water meters, responding to fire or police incidents, answering phone calls and requests from citizens). For instance, a city with 10,000 citizens requires more city employees than a city with 1000 citizens. Thus, a + (same) is at the head of the arrow from *Citizens* to *Regular*

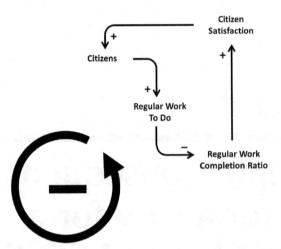

Figure 4.1 Balancing loop for citizen satisfaction.

Work To Do representing that these variables move in the same direction. As one increases, the other increases. Or, vice versa, as one decreases, the other decreases. Next, the *Regular Work To Do* impacts the *Regular Work Completion Ratio*. The *Regular Work Completion Ratio* is the comparison of how much work has been completed and how much work is sitting in the backlog (waiting to be done). If we put this in a ratio format, the *Regular Work Completed* (shown in a later feedback loop, Figure 4.7) would be in the numerator of the ratio (on the top of the fraction), and the *Regular Work To Do* would be in the denominator of the ratio (on the bottom of the fraction). If the *Regular Work Completed* equals the *Regular Work To Do*, the ratio is exactly 1. Assuming the amount of *Regular Work Completed* each time segment (e.g., day, week) stays constant, then as the *Regular Work To Do* increases, the *Regular Work Completion Ratio* decreases (because the value on the bottom of the fraction gets bigger relative to the value on the top of the fraction). And, vice versa, as the *Regular Work To Do* decreases, the *Regular Work Completion Ratio* increases (because the value on the bottom of the fraction gets smaller relative to the value on the top of the fraction). This relationship is represented with the − (opposite) at the head of the arrow from *Regular Work To Do* to *Regular Work Completion Ratio*, indicating that the variables move in opposite directions. The *Regular Work Completion Ratio* then impacts *Citizen Satisfaction*, and these variables move in the same direction. The higher the *Regular Work Completion Ratio* (indicating that all the work is getting done and no work is delayed), the higher the *Citizen Satisfaction* because the citizens are getting their municipal needs adequately met. Conversely, the lower the *Regular Work Completion Ratio* (indicating that work is piling up and taking longer and longer to complete), the lower the *Citizen Satisfaction* because the citizens are not getting their municipal needs met adequately. Things are taking longer, and the quality of the work is lower. Finally, the *Citizen Satisfaction* level comes back around to impact the number of *Citizens*. By the + (same) sign at the head of the arrow from *Citizen Satisfaction* to *Citizens*, we see that these variables move in the same direction. The higher the *Citizen Satisfaction*, the more *Citizens* there will be (over time) due to the positive word of mouth from the current citizens, positive news reports, public accolades, and so on that attract new citizens. In addition, the current citizens stay and perhaps build larger families, or children grow up and decide to stay in the city and raise their own families. However, if *Citizen Satisfaction* is low, this can decrease the number of *Citizens* as current citizens move away and discourage others from coming, and so on.

If we count the – (opposite) signs in the feedback loop, there is an odd number (i.e., only one), which is our indication that this is a balancing (or negative) feedback loop. Essentially, the number of *Citizens* is balanced by whatever level of work the employees in the city can accomplish (via the *Regular Work Completion Ratio*). The more work that can be accomplished by city employees, the higher the *Customer Satisfaction*, and the population in the city will tend to grow over time. Or, if the city staff is insufficient and cannot get work done (resulting in long delays and disappointment), then the population will tend to shrink over time. [Note: Of course, there are many things that influence whether citizens stay or leave a city. But, for the purposes of this particular consequence map, we simplify the situation and are only considering the level of satisfaction as a driver.]

Figure 4.2 shows the reinforcing feedback loop due to employee motivation. Similar to the *Regular Work Completion Ratio* shown in Figure 4.1, there is an *Improvement Work Completion Ratio* that is dependent on the amount of *Improvement Work Completed*. (In this consequence map, there are two major types of work that can be done: regular work, and improvement work aimed at making the organization's processes more effective and efficient.) The dependency is shown by a + (same) sign at the head of the arrow from *Improvement Work Completed* to *Improvement Work Completion Ratio*, indicating that these variables move in the same direction. The *Improvement Work Completion Ratio* then drives the *Improvement Project Success* (in the same direction). In a broad sense, the more improvement-related work that is completed, the more successful the improvement-related projects are.

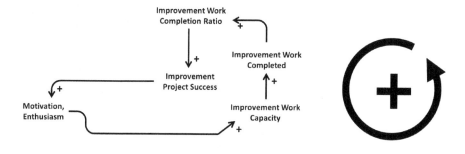

Figure 4.2   Reinforcing loop for employee motivation.

Or, conversely, the less improvement-related work that is completed, the less successful the improvement-related projects are. The success of the improvement projects then has a corresponding impact on the *Motivation, Enthusiasm* of the city staff. These move in the same direction (+ sign at the arrowhead). The more successful the improvement projects are, the more excited and motivated the city staff become. This additional *Motivation, Enthusiasm* then drives the city staff to be more engaged and participate on more improvement projects, thereby increasing the *Improvement Work Capacity*. Or, conversely, if there are not many improvement project successes, then *Motivation, Enthusiasm* will be lower and will tend to make people less excited to tackle more improvement projects (which leads to less *Improvement Work Capacity*). There are no – (opposite) signs in this feedback loop, so it is a reinforcing (or positive) feedback loop that drives changes in the same direction. More begets more, or less begets less. More successful improvement work leads to more excitement, motivation, and enthusiasm to do more improvement work, or the opposite case in which less successful improvement work leads to less excitement, motivation, and enthusiasm to do less improvement work.

Next, we have the reinforcing (or positive) feedback loop for employee productivity shown in Figure 4.3. This feedback loop is an extension of the previous feedback loop in Figure 4.2 for employee motivation, and many of the elements are the same. The primary additions to this feedback loop from the previous feedback loop are *Productivity* and *Total Work Capacity*. In the lower right of Figure 4.3, *Total Work Capacity* influences *Improvement Work Capacity*. The more *Total Work Capacity* there is, then it follows that there will be some more *Improvement Work Capacity*, and vice versa. And, *Productivity* has an influence on *Total Work Capacity*. Given the same amount of human resources, if these resources are more productive, their work capacity increases. Conversely, if their average productivity decreases and the number of resources stay the same, then their work capacity decreases.

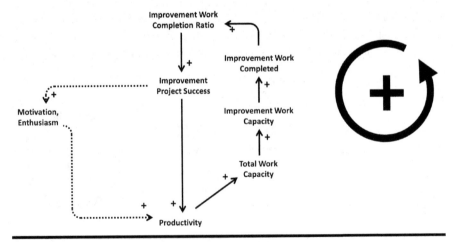

Figure 4.3 Reinforcing loop for employee productivity.

Imagine a quick example in which there are 10 people working 8 hours each day with an average productivity of 1. This provides the equivalent of 80 hours of work each day (10 people × 8 hours/person × 1.0 = 80 hours). If their average productivity increased to 1.25, there would be the equivalent of 100 hours of work each day (10 people × 8 hours/person × 1.25 = 100 hours). On the other hand, if their average productivity dropped to 0.75 (i.e., 75% as productive as they previously were), there would be an equivalent of 60 hours of work each day (10 people × 8 hours/person × 0.75 = 60 hours). The feedback loop in 4.3 adds a connection from *Motivation, Enthusiasm* to *Productivity*. Not only does an increase in *Motivation, Enthusiasm* increase the city staff's desire to do more improvement projects, the increase in *Motivation, Enthusiasm* can also make them more productive, which leads to an increase in *Total Work Capacity*. Furthermore, when there are successful improvement projects, it means that improvements are being implemented, which improves productivity. Improvements allow us to do more work with less resources (or the same amount of resources). This, of course, is why we do improvement projects: to do better. Thus, we see a + (same) arrow going from *Improvement Project Success* to *Productivity*. Similar to the previous feedback loop in 4.2, there are no − (opposite) signs, so this feedback loop is a reinforcing (or positive) feedback loop where improvements drive *Productivity* which increases work capacity to do more improvements.

The reader will notice that once we start drawing a few of the feedback loops, there is significant overlap among the feedback loops such that each new feedback loop builds a little more onto a previous feedback loop. That is the case with the feedback loop in Figure 4.4, also. The reinforcing (or positive) feedback loop in Figure 4.4 adds another element that has an impact on *Motivation, Enthusiasm* that was introduced in Figures 4.2 and 4.3. In Figure 4.4, *Management Support*

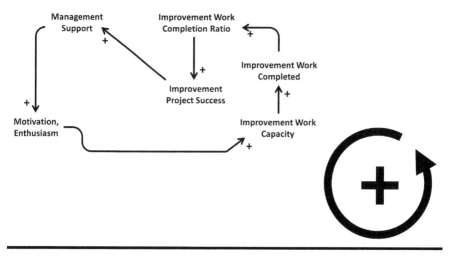

Figure 4.4   Reinforcing loop for management support and motivation.

has an impact on *Motivation, Enthusiasm*. When there is visible and tangible support from management for some new activity or behavior, generally it increases the *Motivation, Enthusiasm* of the employees to continue doing the new activity or behavior. Conversely, when it looks like management does not care or does not like a new activity or behavior, the employees' motivation to continue that activity or behavior will generally decline over time. Something that impacts the *Management Support* is the perceived success rate of the new activity or behavior. In this case, the new activity or behavior is Lean Six Sigma (i.e., process improvements), so there is a + (same) arrow from *Improvement Project Success* to *Management Support*. The more that management sees the improvement projects succeed and generate good results, the more support the management will show toward the efforts, which makes the employees (city staff) more excited and motivated to continue the improvement projects. This completes the reinforcing (or positive) feedback loop.

The feedback loop in Figure 4.5 is an extension of the feedback loop in Figure 4.4, which brings in *Productivity*, as in Figure 4.3. This reinforcing (or positive) feedback loop indicates that *Management Support* can result in increased *Productivity* through higher *Motivation, Enthusiasm*. Then, of course, the rest of the feedback loop shows that increases in *Productivity* create higher work capacity, which can be used to conduct improvement projects.

The feedback loop in Figure 4.6 adds three elements to the core of Figure 4.2. On the left of the diagram, another element that affects the *Improvement Work Capacity* is the level of *Improvement Skills*. If the city staff learns more about how to improve processes within the city and which improvement tools and techniques to use, the average "skill level" of the city staff increases with regard to improvement projects. As with all + (same) relationships, the converse is also true. If the city staff's *Improvement Skills* decreases, the *Improvement Work Capacity* will also decrease.

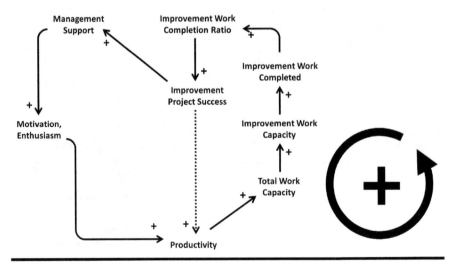

Figure 4.5 Reinforcing loop for management support and productivity.

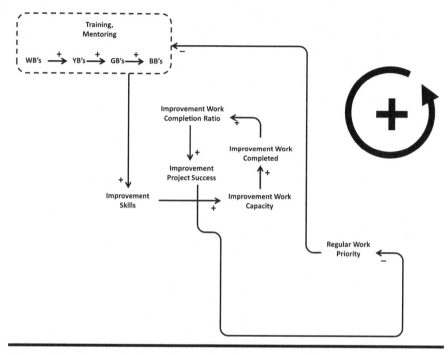

Figure 4.6   Reinforcing loop for training increase from improvements.

The driver of the city staff's Improvement Skills is the Lean Six Sigma *Training, Mentoring*. Within the box of *Training, Mentoring* there is a progression from White Belt (WB) to Yellow Belt (YB) to Green Belt (GB) to Black Belt (BB), indicating the maturation of the city staff as they receive more *Training, Mentoring*. Thus, the more *Training, Mentoring* that the city staff completes, the higher the average *Improvement Skills* of the city staff. The other additional element in Figure 4.6 is the level of *Regular Work Priority*. This works in opposition to the improvement projects. The more priority that is given to doing regular work, the less priority will be given to improvement projects. In other words, the focus becomes doing the day-to-day activities instead of stepping back and taking time to analyze and improve the day-to-day activities. This is very typical within many organizations. As shown by the – arrow from *Improvement Project Success* to *Regular Work Priority*, the less success there is with improvements, the higher the priority will be for regular work. That is, management will tend to say that the improvements are not doing anything, so skip them and do the "real" day-to-day work. Of course, the converse holds true with this – (opposite) relationship as well. If *Improvement Project Success* increases, then there will be a tendency by management to relax the *Regular Work Priority* because they are seeing value in doing the improvements. Last of all (and this is the killer of many new initiatives), the *Regular Work Priority* can influence how much *Training, Mentoring* occurs. The – (opposite) arrow indicates that an increase in *Regular Work*

Priority will create a decrease in the *Training, Mentoring* as management uses time and money to do "real" work instead of more training. In fact, when budgets get tight, one of the first areas that often gets cut in organizations is the training budget because no "immediate" benefit can be seen. The return-on-investment payback period is too long and the organization cannot afford to wait that long. As always, the converse is also true. A decrease in the *Regular Work Priority* can result in an increase in the *Training, Mentoring*. If we count the – signs in the loop, we find and even number of – signs (two of them). These counteract each other so that we end up with a reinforcing (positive) feedback loop. In this feedback loop, an increase in *Training, Mentoring* leads to an increase in *Improvement Skills* which increases the *Improvement Work Capacity*, and eventually the *Improvement Project Success* allows the *Regular Work Priority* to decrease, which allows for an increase in more *Training, Mentoring*, and the cycle continues. Or, the cycle can work in the opposite direction. If *Regular Work Priority* is high, then there is little *Training, Mentoring* (for Lean Six Sigma or whatever the newly desired activity or behavior is) which causes a decrease in skills and a decrease in good results, which then causes the *Regular Work Priority* to increase again.

Figure 4.7 builds on Figure 4.6 a great deal. Now, we begin to see more of the other elements that have been hinted at so far. For example, on the right side of the diagram, there are elements for regular work that match some of the elements for improvement work. There is a *Regular Work Capacity* that results in *Regular Work Completed*, which drives the *Regular Work Completion Ratio*. Both *Regular Work*

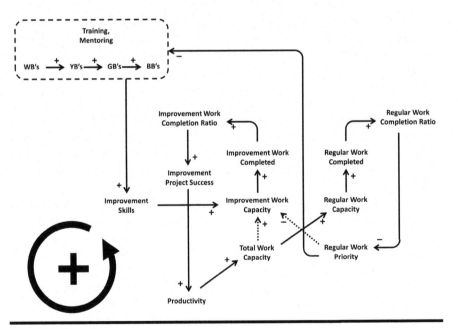

Figure 4.7   Reinforcing loop for training increase from productivity.

Capacity and *Improvement Work Capacity* are driven by the *Total Work Capacity*. At any point in time, the organization has the choice of putting some of its work capacity toward regular day-to-day work or toward improvement work (i.e., spending time to analyze current processes and make changes to those processes). As *Total Work Capacity* increases, those increases can be shared between the *Regular Work Capacity* and the *Improvement Work Capacity*. The *Regular Work Completion Ratio* then impacts the *Regular Work Priority* with a – (opposite) relationship. As the *Regular Work Completion Ratio* increases, it indicates that there are sufficient resources for addressing the day-to-day activities of the city. This relaxes the *Regular Work Priority*. However, if the opposite is true and the *Regular Work Completion Ratio* is low, there is an increase in the *Regular Work Priority* because there are clearly not enough resources to cover even the day-to-day work, much less any improvement work. This is represented by the – (opposite) arrow going from *Regular Work Priority* to *Improvement Work Capacity*. When the *Regular Work Priority* is high, the amount of capacity given to improvement projects is low. And, when the *Regular Work Priority* is low, the amount of capacity given to improvement projects can be higher.

Figure 4.8 adds one very realistic element to the feedback loops so far. On the left side of the diagram, notice that an increase in *Training, Mentoring* leads to a decrease in *Total Work Capacity*. When employees are in training, they are not available to do the day-to-day work. If we take this to the extreme, if employees were put in training classes all the time to increase their skill levels, the day-to-day work would never get done, and the organization would fall apart. This creates a balancing (or negative) feedback loop that says the *Training, Mentoring* will

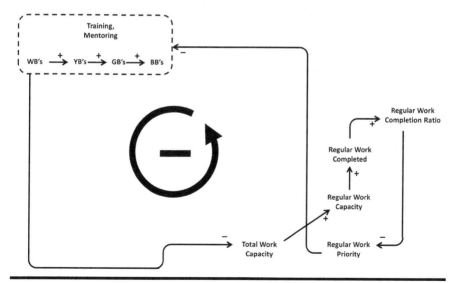

Figure 4.8   Balancing loop for training decrease.

only occur at the level that the organization can continue to keep its *Regular Work Completion Ratio* at a sufficient level. Notice that this is only the second balancing (or negative) feedback loop we have seen so far in this system. The first balancing feedback loop is in Figure 4.1. The other six figures in between have been reinforcing (or positive) feedback loops. This is very common in organizations. There are many "growth" feedback loops with only a few management "control" loops that try to maintain some sort of balance among a few elements (regardless if that management is done knowingly or unknowingly).

The feedback loop in Figure 4.9 builds on the concept of regular work and adds the real-world element of *Fatigue*, which has a negative impact on *Productivity*. The more fatigued someone is, the less productive they are. Perhaps not immediately, but eventually fatigue will slow a person down so that they are not at full mental and physical capacity. If the *Regular Work Completion Ratio* is low (on the right side of the diagram), it means that there are insufficient resources for doing the day-to-day work. In lieu of hiring more staff (which takes time), the typical short-term reaction from management is to work people overtime, thereby increasing the *Average Hours Per Day* that they work. Instead, if the *Regular Work Completion Ratio* is high, it means that there are more than enough resources to do the day-to-day work. Therefore, management can allow people to work fewer hours (as opposed to laying off people). Now, of course, the employees may never be allowed to work a shorter day than normal (say, perhaps an 8-hour day), but any overtime would be removed and there would be an easier work environment. Even though people may still be there 8 hours each day, the intensity of those 8 hours has diminished. The *Average Hours Per Day* then has a direct impact on *Fatigue*. With the +

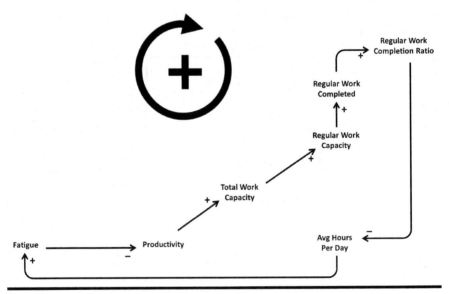

Figure 4.9 Reinforcing loop for employee fatigue.

(same) relationship, the higher the *Average Hours Per Day*, the higher the *Fatigue* (and the lower the *Productivity*). Conversely, the lower the *Average Hours Per Day*, the lower the *Fatigue* (and the higher the *Productivity*). In total, this is a reinforcing (or positive) feedback loop because there are two – (opposite) signs that counteract each other, and it works like this: A low *Regular Work Completion Ratio* results in more work hours per day for employees, which increases *Fatigue* and decreases *Productivity*. A decrease in *Productivity* drives down the *Total Work Capacity*, which then causes less regular work to be done, which only makes the *Regular Work Completion Ratio* decrease again.

Figure 4.10 incorporates the *Motivation, Enthusiasm* from earlier figures and adds *Turnover* and *Staff* to the system. On the left side of the diagram, as *Fatigue* increases (due to an increase in *Average Hours Per Day* for employees), it decreases the *Motivation, Enthusiasm* of the employees. This can result in *Turnover* (i.e., employees leaving the organization). The – (opposite) sign indicates this. The lower the *Motivation, Enthusiasm*, the higher the *Turnover*. Or the converse: the higher the *Motivation, Enthusiasm*, the lower the *Turnover* (i.e., people are excited to stay at the organization). The number of *Staff* (i.e., people) has a direct relationship to the *Total Work Capacity*. The more *Staff*, the higher the *Total Work Capacity*, and vice versa. This reinforcing (or positive) feedback loops signifies that a low *Regular Work Completion Ratio* will result in a higher *Average Hours Per Day* for the staff, which will increase *Fatigue*, decrease *Motivation, Enthusiasm*, and increase *Turnover*. The increased *Turnover* will reduce the *Staff* and *Total Work Capacity*, which then results in less regular work getting done and a decrease in the *Regular Work Completion Ratio*.

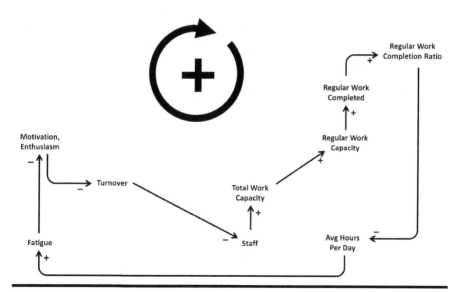

Figure 4.10   Reinforcing loop for employee turnover.

The Full Consequence Map

Figure 4.11 pulls all the previous feedback loops together and adds a few more connections among the elements. Notice that with these additional connections, even more feedback loops could be drawn. However, in this case, most of the key feedback loops are covered in the previous figures. The additional connections and possible additional feedback loops will end up being very similar to the feedback loops already presented. Here are some of the additional connections.

- The *Total Work Capacity* is a combination of how many *Staff* there are as well as the *Average Hours Per Day* that they work and the average level of *Productivity*.
- *Management Support* (of the new activity or behavior, in this case, Lean Six Sigma activities) has an inversely proportional effect on *Regular Work Priority*. If *Management Support* for the new activity is high, then the *Regular Work Priority* will be lower than normal.
- *Motivation, Enthusiasm* has a proportional effect on *Training, Mentoring*. The more excited the organization becomes, the more people will make themselves available to go through training for the new skill.

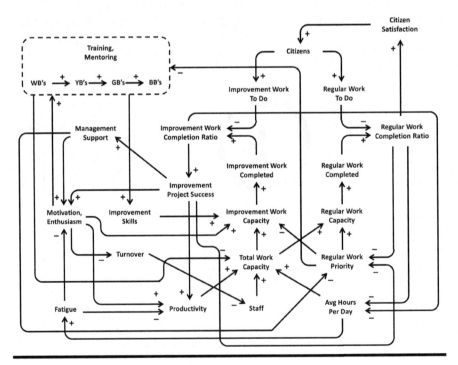

Figure 4.11   Combined feedback loops in consequence map.

∎ *Improvement Project Success* has an inversely proportional effect on *Regular Work Priority*. If *Improvement Project Success* is high, then the *Regular Work Priority* will be lower than normal because people will want to do more improvement work.

∎ The amount of *Citizens* drives the amount of *Improvement Work To Do* in the same way that the amount of *Citizens* drives the amount of *Regular Work To Do*. And, the *Improvement Work To Do* has the same connection to the *Improvement Work Completion Ratio* (that mirrors the connection of the *Regular Work To Do* to the *Regular Work Completion Ratio*).

Now that all the feedback loops have been explained individually, it is easy to see how complicated a structure can get for any given system. And, it becomes painfully clear that there is no single, silver bullet solution. You cannot do just "one thing." Each element is part of multiple feedback loops, with some feedback loops supporting each other and some feedback loops working in opposition to each other. Some feedback loops operate over a very short time frame, and some feedback loops operate over a much longer time frame. Some feedback loops are very strong, and some feedback loops are weak. For example, consider *Productivity*. It appears in four of the feedback loops presented earlier in this chapter. Looking at Figure 4.11, *Productivity* has three elements that impact it (*Improvement Project Success*, *Motivation, Enthusiasm*, and *Fatigue*), and it impacts one element (*Total Work Capacity*). Changes in *Productivity* due to *Improvement Project Success* will take a long time to come into fruition because the improvement projects have to be conducted and completed, which can take weeks or months. However, changes in *Productivity* due to *Fatigue* are very quick. When someone is heavily fatigued, the drop in *Productivity* happens immediately.

In fact, most disagreements about management or organizational policies come from two people (or two parties) having different underlying models of the system structure. Each person (or party) can only see part of the system, so they form a model that has their known part of the system. However, rarely is it the entire system. Instead of arguing about the exact policy, we should argue about the elements and connections in the underlying model. Once the model is agreed upon, in my experience, the correct policy usually becomes very clear.

In this particular example with the city and their implementation of Lean Six Sigma, we focused on the areas highlighted in Figure 4.12:

∎ Training, Mentoring
∎ Management Support
∎ Staff
∎ Average Hours Per Day
∎ Regular Work Priority

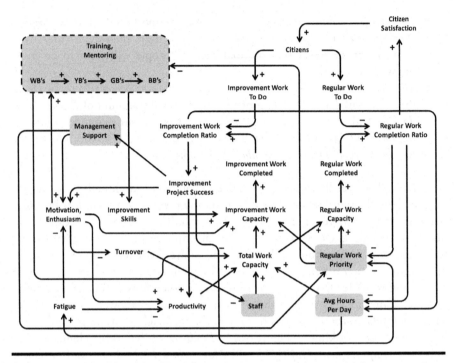

Figure 4.12   Combined feedback loops in consequence map with leverage points.

We focused on these elements because these were within city management control at the time. In other words, the city managers could alter any of these elements directly. For instance, the city managers could directly increase Lean Six Sigma *Training, Mentoring,* if desired. They could hire a consultant to come in and do training or even purchase some online training for employees. As another example, the city managers could directly increase their level of *Management Support* for Lean Six Sigma by attending team meetings, attending training, recognizing individual and team efforts, and so on.

Even though these elements are part of multiple feedback loops, they can be directly changed, if desired. Of course, keep in mind that the changes will drive other changes throughout the connected feedback loops, so these additional impacts needed to be considered. However, change needs to start somewhere. If the system is ever going to change, it has to be "perturbed" in a few places to "jump start" the parts of the system that have been dormant or are weaker/slower than other feedback loops. For this particular system and issue, we identified five possible places to do this. Now, the task was understanding how to change these five elements so that the desired behavior would occur. Which should be increased, and which should be decreased? What are the ripple effects through the other feedback loops? Can we live with those ripple effects?

What Does the Consequence Map Show Us?

The previous section introduced the five elements in the city organizational system that could be directly influenced by the city management:

- Training, Mentoring
- Management Support
- Staff
- Average Hours per Day
- Regular Work Priority

In many systems for many situations, making a single change typically does not lead to the desired system performance. Usually, multiple actions are required at different parts of the system. In other words, multiple policies are needed simultaneously.

In this example with the city, we have seen that there are positive feedback loops that drive the improvement process so that it continues to grow: More improvement work leads to more *Improvement Project Success*, which increases *Productivity* and allows more *Total Work Capacity* to be allocated to improvement projects, which then repeats the cycle. It can be a virtuous loop (a reinforcing loop that drives behavior in the desired direction) or a vicious loop (a reinforcing loop that drives behavior in the opposite direction than the desired direction). We want the loop to become a virtuous loop that sustains itself over time. However, that is not the current situation, so a catalyst is needed to kick start the system in the right direction. This is where the five elements play a role.

First, city management can increase Lean Six Sigma *Training, Mentoring* by offering on-site training using a consultant. Over time, this will increase the *Improvement Skills* of the city staff, which increases the amount of improvement work that can be done by the staff. The key is that the *Training, Mentoring* cannot be a one-time shot. It has to continue for a period of time to allow the stronger, more sustainable "improvement" loop to kick in and take over.

Second, city management can augment *Staff* by bringing in outside consultants with Lean Six Sigma skills to help run projects, as well as temporary labor to help cover daily tasks for the people that are going to training and spending time on Lean Six Sigma projects. Again, this staff augmentation will need to continue for a period of time to allow the improvement loop to kick in. If staff is increased for just 1 day or 1 week it will not be enough, and no change will occur.

Third, in conjunction with adding *Staff*, city management can authorize some overtime (as needed) to help staff get the first couple of improvement projects under their belts. That is, city management can increase the *Average Hours Per Day* for the staff. When implementing a new activity like Lean Six Sigma, employees are usually too busy with their current day-to-day activities and tasks to carve out time to work on improvement projects. A typical saying is that "it is difficult to drain the swamp when you are up to your waist in alligators." By providing authorization for paid overtime, these employees can feel like they are getting something for their time. In most cases, employees are excited to try to make the organization better and are willing to spend some time on it. However, one of the biggest killers of new initiatives like Lean Six Sigma is to expect employees to "do it on their own time." This is a very short-sighted solution that will ultimately fail. What kind of message does that send? It says that management doesn't care, so why should the employees. If the organization wants to make the change, then the organization needs to back it with money to prove the organization is serious.

Fourth, city management must decrease the *Regular Work Priority* to allow people to take time to go to training and work on improvement projects. If management continues to scream at employees for occasionally skipping daily work to conduct analysis and brainstorm how make the organization better, then the employees will obviously not bother to do anything other than the daily work ... in the same inefficient way it has always been done.

Finally, and most importantly, the city managers must show *Management Support* for Lean Six Sigma and all the improvement activities. This is the easiest, yet most difficult, change to make because it requires a significant change of behavior on behalf of the individual managers. Why do I say the change is "significant?" Because if the change was not significant, it would have already been done. Managers must constantly show approval for the Lean Six Sigma training and activities by attending the training themselves, participating on improvement teams themselves, visiting other team meetings, praising the results of improvement projects, leaning on other department heads that are not "getting on board with it," and so on. Employees must see that management "has their backs" and approves of the additional time and work it will take to get the improvement feedback loop going.

If these five actions are sustained over a period of a few months, it allows the improvement feedback loops to dominate the system and drive new results. In the systems approach, rarely is the behavior in the short term the same as the behavior in the long term. Consequently, rarely are actions taken that produce good short-term results the same actions that will produce good long-term results. These actions are typically opposite: Actions that produce good short-term results will create poor long-term results, and actions that produce good long-term results will create poor short-term results. The challenge for management is to push through the poor short-term results so that the good long-term results are realized. No pain, no gain. This means that for new initiatives (in this case the new initiative is Lean Six Sigma but it can be any new initiative), the organization may need some additional help to kick start the initiative and keep feeding it while the longer-term feedback loops begin to kick in and get stronger. And, upper management plays a big role by showing support and continuing to push the agenda. It cannot be a single event. Like dieting, it requires discipline and time. Rome wasn't built in a day.

Final Remarks

In this particular example with the city, the city did not get it right the first time around. Instead, the first time that the city tried to implement Lean Six Sigma, the city suffered the same common fate as most organizations. There was a lot of buzz and attention at first, but then things died down and everyone returned to doing the same things they always did. It was a fad, and there was no permanent change. With the creation of the consequence map in Figure 4.12, the city managers learned from the first initiative that they themselves played a key role that was not fulfilled (e.g., *Management Support*) and that they had several "levers" that they could pull for the system to make some direct changes. So, the city decided to try again. And, for the second initiative, they are doing much better. At the time of this publication, the stronger improvement feedback loops have not kicked in 100%, but they are ramping up and getting stronger each month. A few key processes have been improved, and the city is realizing the benefits of these improvements with better results (which provides reinforcement for continuing the activities). Essentially, the city is far enough along that it is becoming a benchmark example for other cities on how to implement improvement initiatives. There is the realization that this takes sustained attention and effort for a period of time, and the city managers are providing that through the five elements mentioned in the previous section. There is a great deal of confidence that they are on their way to sustaining this initiative. It has been a joy to work with the city management, and I can see that they are on the right track. They are in it for the long haul, and it shows.

Let me end by stating that, even though this consequence map has been very helpful, this consequence map is by no means complete. The questions or issues posed to an organization at a particular point in time drive the scope of the consequence map. In this case, we were looking at a specific change initiative and why it struggled on the first attempt and, therefore, how to do it better on the second attempt. For this purpose, the consequence map in Figure 4.2 was extremely helpful and useful. Yet, the consequence map could easily be expanded. For instance, in the current consequence map there is no limit on the size of the population. In reality, geographic, political, economic, and other constraints can limit the population size. As an extreme example, consider a city that is only 1 square mile in area. A city with this little land cannot possibly sustain 10 million citizens. This specific constraint was not considered in the consequence map, along with many other constraints that were outside the scope of consideration for the issue.

When building consequence maps, you want just enough scope to adequately cover the situation at hand and all the relevant elements and variables that might play a role. But, you do not want to try to create the mega-consequence map that includes the entire world. It is not feasible. As you build consequence maps, you will begin to learn where the appropriate "line in the sand" is for your issues that will indicate when you have enough scope. One piece of advice: If you build a consequence map that does not adequately cover your issue or problem, then most likely you need to continue to expand the scope of the map. So, always try to start small. Then, grow and expand the map a little bit at a time, continually checking if you have all the major feedback loops that impact your system.

Chapter 5

Example Consequence Map for a Non-Profit Organization for Grant Proposals

This chapter walks through the specific use of consequence mapping to understand the short-term and long-term consequences of activities that occur during the grant proposal writing process at a non-profit organization. Many non-profits rely on grants to pay for operating expenses, so the grant proposal writing process is extremely important. In this example, the non-profit seemed to suffer from a slow degradation of the quality (and success) of its grant proposals over several years. Essentially, they were not as successful as they had previously been, which had a significant impact on operations that resulted in a reduction of the workforce. That reduction in workforce, of course, caused a decrease in the capacity of the non-profit to provide services to its clients. It would require a larger consequence map to look at the entire system that includes both proposal writing and service delivery. For simplicity, we initially focused on the grant proposal writing "system" with the understanding that we might need to expand our analysis if the scope of activities were not enough to drive any significant changes and improvements. As it turned out, developing a consequence map for the proposal writing process was sufficient for this project.

The Full Consequence Map

For this chapter, we will start with the overall completed consequence map and then describe the key feedback loops that drive the system. This is opposite from the approach in Chapter 4 to the city consequence map for Lean Six Sigma (or any major change initiative), in which we walked through the individual feedback loops first and then showed the entire system. Figure 5.2 shows the completed consequence map for the overall system that was analyzed. It is the grant proposal writing process for the non-profit. However, before discussing Figure 5.2, let us begin with Figure 5.1.

Figure 5.1 shows the initial consequence map, which provided a very high-level view of the vicious loop from which the non-profit suffered. In the feedback loop, *Resource Capacity* determines the level of *Resource Availability*. (Note that these variables hold for whatever activity, be it proposal writing or service delivery.) There is an S for the arrow, which indicates that the variables move in the same direction: an increase in *Resource Capacity* increases the *Resource Availability* (or a decrease in *Resource Capacity* decreases the *Resource Availability*). The *Resource Availability* then impacts who is available for *Reviews/Meetings* (e.g., review of the proposal content). There is an S for this arrow, so the number of and attendance at *Review/Meetings* moves in the same direction as the *Resource Availability*. The number of *Reviews/Meetings* has an opposite effect on *Rework* (as indicated by the O at the head of the arrow from *Review/Meetings* to *Rework*). Thus, the more *Reviews/Meetings* there are, the less *Rework* there is. In this sense, *Rework* means corrective work, not the regular proposal work. In other words, the more opportunities that more key people in the organization (e.g., management) have to see the content of the proposal, the more opportunities these people have to provide input or edits that will prevent massive rework efforts later because the proposal got too far along in the process before someone caught a mistake, for example. Or, more relevant to the current situation for this non-profit, if there are fewer *Reviews/Meetings* (or less attendance at those *Reviews/Meetings*), then the amount of *Rework* increases, because the details of the proposal are not being discussed adequately until a "due date" is rapidly approaching or some other formal deadline forces a serious review or meeting to occur. This is a very common

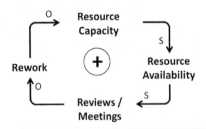

Figure 5.1   Reinforcing loop for rework and capacity constraints.

dynamic for organizations. Many times, the appropriate people from management or another group or department within the organization are not available for the "regular" proposal reviews, so the proposal continues along the same path. Later, when a "formal" proposal review occurs that requires mandatory attendance of all the key decision makers and input providers, suddenly there are major changes, because these people are finally getting a chance to see the proposal contents. Unfortunately, most of these changes could have been caught much sooner in a regular proposal review had the key people attended as planned. The increase in *Rework* caused by the lack of attendance at *Reviews/Meetings* then decreases (i.e., takes away from) the *Resource Capacity* for writing proposals, and the loop continues again. Notice that this is a positive (reinforcing) feedback loop, because there is an even number of Os in the loop (in this case, two Os).

As stated earlier in this chapter, this non-profit suffered from the vicious side of the feedback loop: the loop worked in the opposite direction from what they wanted. In the vicious loop, a low level of *Resource Capacity* for writing proposals caused a decrease in *Resource Availability* for *Reviews/Meetings*, which then added more *Rework* and stripped the *Resource Capacity* even more, which made it even more difficult to attend *Reviews/Meetings* and caused more *Rework*, and so on. This is the overall feedback loop that we started with. The next step was to go into a deeper level of detail and expand the loop (Figure 5.2).

In Figure 5.2, begin in the upper right part of the graphic with *Proposal Work*. In this non-profit organization, as with many organizations, there is not a full-time staff of proposal writers. There may be one "proposal leader" who is dedicated to the project, but typically, people from the "normal line of work" for the organization are pulled together for the proposal project. Unfortunately, in many of these cases, the *Standard Work* must also continue while the *Proposal Work* moves along. Thus, employees often struggle to balance these two workloads, which combine to make up their total workload (*Employee Workload*). There is a dotted line from *Proposal Work* to *Standard Work* to indicate that, over time with a delay, successful proposals eventually result in new work for the organization. The Ss indicate that the variables move in the same direction. For example, the more *Proposal Work*

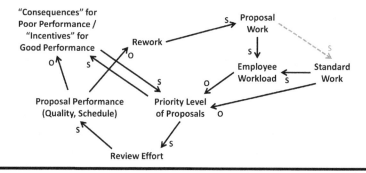

Figure 5.2 Full consequence map for proposal process.

there is, the more total work (*Employee Workload*) there is. The *Employee Workload* and *Standard Work* tend to have an opposite effect on the *Priority Level of Proposals* (denoted by the O on the arrowheads), because people usually prefer to do the *Standard Work* of the organization (the "real" work) in lieu of the *Proposal Work*, or management prefers employees to do the *Standard Work* (and, thus, put indirect pressure on them to favor the *Standard Work* over the *Proposal Work*). In fact, in some organizations, employees feel a little as if they are being "punished" when they are assigned to a proposal team, as if they were not good enough to do the real work of the organization. As a result, they often consider proposal work a low priority. Or, at the other extreme, only the top employees are assigned to the proposal team. But, top employees are always in high demand for the *Standard Work*, so, again, they will tend to put a lower priority on the *Proposal Work* in favor of the real *Standard Work*.

The *Priority Level of Proposals* causes a change in the same direction (S at arrowhead) for the amount of *Review Effort* (i.e., meetings, reviews, etc. to look at how the proposal is progressing). The higher the *Priority of the Proposals*, the more *Review Effort* there tends to be. Conversely, the lower the *Priority of the Proposals* (as is typically the case and was, indeed, the case with this non-profit), the less *Review Effort* there tends to be. The level of *Review Effort* impacts the *Proposal Performance* (i.e., the quality of the proposal, the timeliness of the proposal to meet the due dates) in a similar way. The more *Review Effort* there is, the better the *Proposal Performance* in terms of meeting due dates and creating a high-quality proposal that stands a good chance of winning the grant. Conversely, the less *Review Effort* there is, the worse the *Proposal Performance* is. The *Proposal Performance* then has an effect in the opposite direction for *Rework*. The better the *Proposal Performance* (i.e., the better the quality of the proposal content), the less *Rework* is required. On the other hand, the worse the *Proposal Performance*, the more *Rework* is required to get the quality of the proposal back up to par. *Rework*, of course, then drives the amount of *Proposal Work* in the same direction (S on the arrow), and the feedback loop starts over again.

The Feedback Loops

Figure 5.3 highlights this reinforcing (positive) feedback loop (even number of Os). A high *Employee Workload* (driven by *Proposal Work*) causes a low *Priority Level of Proposals* (in favor of *Standard Work*), which results in less *Review Effort*, worse *Proposal Performance*, and more *Rework*, which adds to the *Employee Workload* to start the cycle over again.

Figure 5.4 highlights a balancing (negative) feedback loop that represents management's control of the grant proposal writing process or system. A variable for *Consequences and Incentives* is highlighted. This represents the various ways in which management provides negative consequences for poor *Proposal Performance*.

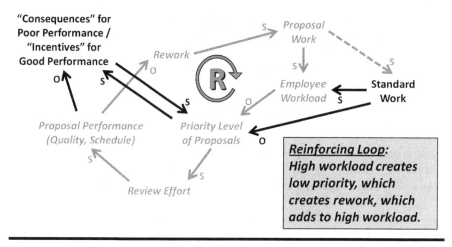

Figure 5.3   Reinforcing loop for proposal rework and employee workload.

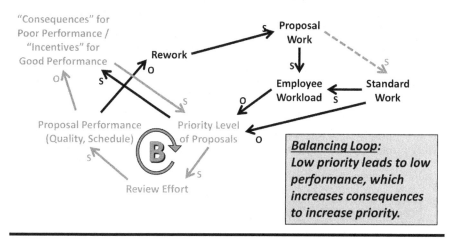

Figure 5.4   Balancing loop for prioritization and consequences.

This can range anywhere from criticizing the proposal team members publicly during a large staff meeting to taking away perks such as paid overtime. The *Consequences and Incentives* variable also represents the various ways in which management provides incentives for good *Proposal Performance*. This can range anywhere from throwing celebration parties for the proposal team to informal kudos or compliments from key management personnel. Notice that the arrow from *Proposal Performance* to *Consequences and Incentives* has an O on it. This means that the lower the *Proposal Performance* (i.e., lower quality), the more *Consequences* there will be for poor performance. The higher the *Proposal Performance* (i.e., better quality), the fewer *Consequences* there will be for poor performance. The net effect of this variable is to drive the *Priority Level of Proposals*. When the consequences for poor *Proposal Performance* are high, the *Priority Level of Proposals* tends to increase for the team, because the proposal team members do not want to suffer more consequences. Thus, there is an S on the arrow from *Consequences and Incentives* to *Priority Level of Proposals*. On the other hand, if there are very few consequences for poor *Proposal Performance*, then there will be a low *Priority Level of Proposals*, because there are no "punishments" for doing poorly. The proposal team has no incentive to do better. This is a balancing loop, because there is an odd number of Os (only one). Thus, this loop will tend to try to maintain a certain quality level (via *Proposal Performance*) by implementing *Consequences* to maintain a high *Priority Level of Proposals* so that employees take the proposal work seriously.

Figure 5.5 shows the same feedback loops as Figures 5.3 and 5.4, but Figure 5.5 lays them out a little differently to help with visualization. The reinforcing (positive) feedback loop from Figure 5.3 competes directly with the balancing (negative) feedback loop in Figure 5.4 through the chain of variables *Priority Level of Proposals* to *Review Effort* to *Proposal Performance* (i.e., these three variables are shared by both feedback loops). Notice in Figure 5.5 that the R for the reinforcing loop is much larger than the B for the balancing loop. The intention is to show that the reinforcing loop is currently overpowering the balancing loop. This means that the vicious loop of the high *Employee Workload* lowering the *Priority Level of Proposals* (resulting in worse *Proposal Performance* and more *Rework*) is overpowering the management control balancing feedback loop, which has the purpose of maintaining a high level of quality for proposals (and a high *Priority Level*). With this dynamic, it is easy to see that the proposal writing process will erode over time, so that grant proposal writing becomes less and less important, which results in poor-quality proposals. Consequently, poor-quality proposals stand very little chance of

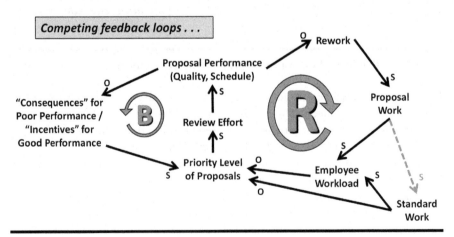

Figure 5.5 Competing feedback loops.

getting funded. This is precisely the dynamics that the non-profit experienced over several years: lower-quality grant proposals leading to fewer grants awarded.

Figure 5.5 shows the expansion of the simpler reinforcing feedback loop in Figure 5.1 with more details. In essence, while Figure 5.1 shows a single feedback loop operating, when we dug into the details, we found another feedback loop (balancing) in the system. But, this balancing feedback loop was so weak that its impact was not felt, and therefore, at a high level, the system seemed to be only a single feedback loop.

Figure 5.6 adds a couple of external elements to the system. External elements are those elements that are not part of the "closed system" being studied. Of course, these elements are part of a larger system, but for the purposes of this analysis, they were considered outside the scope of the system, because we could generate all relevant dynamics from the two feedback loops shown in Figures 5.3 and 5.4. However, for this analysis, we felt that they played a significant role, so we added them. The external elements are *Executive Attention/Priority* and *Management Attention/Priority*. Notice that *Executive Attention/Priority* drives *Management Attention/Priority* in the same direction. (The dotted line indicates that there can sometimes be a delay before management perceives and adjusts to what the executives are doing.) When *Executive Attention/Priority* is high, then *Management Attention/Priority* is high. Conversely, when *Executive Attention/Priority* is low, then *Management Attention/Priority* is low. In this system, "management" represents the level of management that is accountable for the grant proposals being written. "Executive" represents the next higher level of management above the proposal-level management. For this particular non-profit, the executive management was similar to corporate management in a for-profit organization. Executive management oversaw several non-profit organizations, with this particular non-profit organization being only one of them.

Notice in Figure 5.6 that *Executive Attention/Priority* has an impact on the *Consequences and Incentives* (the S at the arrowhead indicates movement in the

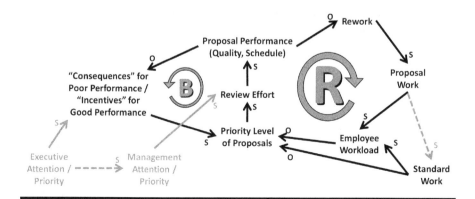

Figure 5.6   External elements.

same direction). As the next level of management above the grant writing process, this executive management has the power, authority, and motivation to control the loop to maintain a certain expected quality level. Also, notice that *Management Attention/Priority* has an impact on the *Review Effort* (the S at the arrowhead indicates movement in the same direction). In fact, the attendance and participation of management in proposal reviews is a key factor in catching mistakes upfront so that they do not create a lot of *Rework* later.

What Does the Consequence Map Show Us?

Most importantly, this consequence map showed the key dynamics that were at play in the system:

- There was a reinforcing (positive) feedback loop that drove the quality of the grant proposals lower because the "real" work of the organization tended to take priority over proposal work.
- There was a balancing (negative) feedback loop for management that attempted to maintain some level of priority and quality for the proposals.
- Unfortunately, the reinforcing feedback loop was a very strong vicious loop that overpowered the management balancing feedback loop. Thus, the quality (and success) of the grant proposals suffered and eroded over time.

Figure 5.7 introduces several opportunities for intervention points in this grant proposal writing system:

- *Executive Attention/Priority*
- *Management Attention/Priority*
- *Shift Standard Work*

These external elements are all within the control of management (or executive management) of the organization. First, executive management can simply give more focus and/or attention to the grant proposal writing process. This can involve "management by walking around" (MBWA), in which they visit the process frequently to show interest and ask questions, or it can involve highlighting proposal writing activities and accomplishments in various management meetings, or any other method for giving attention to the process. Moreover, executive management can also increase the priority of the proposal writing process by emphasizing the importance of the process and successful grants to the non-profit, attending proposal reviews, pushing the layer of management that resides over the proposal process to improve results, and so on. Second, management (the layer of management over the grant proposal writing process) can perform similar activities to those listed for executive management. Third, management can shift some of the regular

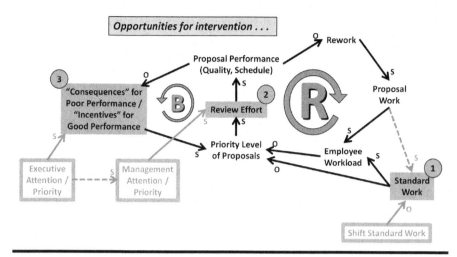

Figure 5.7   Opportunities for intervention in a system.

work of the proposal writing employees off to other resources (either other employees in the organization, contract resources, or volunteers). Shifting the *Standard Work* decreases the total *Employee Workload* and the proportion of *Standard Work* to *Proposal Work*, thereby reducing the priority and pressure of the *Standard Work* to allow the *Proposal Work* to gain a higher priority.

In this particular situation, the non-profit elected to do all three interventions. Executive management began to make occasional appearances in the proposal process and even sit in on some of the proposal reviews. Management made sure to attend all scheduled proposal reviews and meetings, along with sharing performance metrics at larger organization-wide meetings. Finally, management changed the work policies to recruit some additional volunteers to take over more of the day-to-day work of the organization. Anyone participating on a proposal was allowed to shift up to half of their standard workload to the additional volunteers. In addition, three employees were dedicated to the proposal writing process, so that they were engaged in proposal writing full-time. A secondary benefit of this full-time dedication was that proposals were more consistent in terms of style, format, and content, because the same people were involved, so that similar sections from earlier proposals could be used in later proposals with little modification. When the style, format, and contents produced a successful grant, they were duplicated on the next similar grant proposal to increase the probability of success on the next grant. These changes have been in place for only eight months, but the non-profit can already see a significant difference in the flow and organization of the proposal process, along with the quality of proposals. There is often a delay of several months while proposals are evaluated, so only a handful of proposals have been evaluated to see whether these changes had an impact on the success rate of the grant proposals (which, of course, is a primary objective of the consequence mapping project). Of the three proposals that have been evaluated within this short time frame, two have been successful. This is a 67% success rate compared with the 25% success rate that was experienced prior to implementing the changes. Everyone realizes that this is a very small data set for understanding whether the changes had a real impact, but the initial results are extremely positive and higher than anyone expected. As a result, the non-profit intends to continue with the new changes.

In many cases, it takes a while for some of the changes to reap benefits as the longer-term feedback loops kick into gear and begin to dominate the system. In this example with the proposal process for the non-profit, the benefits were recognized fairly quickly. Since executive management had never appeared before, the fact that suddenly, executive management was stopping by made a noticeable difference. Employees even called it the "executive bump" (in reference to Stephen Colbert's "Colbert bump"). This increase in management attention, the participation of management in the reviews, and the relaxation of standard workload for employees participating in the proposal all combined to make a 180-degree turn in the process in a rather short period of time (just a couple of months). This gave people confidence that they were on the right track, which fueled more enthusiasm and motivation for continuing with the new changes. The vicious loop had been successfully reversed into a virtuous loop.

Final Remarks

As with many system structures, the system structure can often be the same from organization to organization. Any reader who has participated in any type of proposal writing for any type of business can probably sympathize with this non-profit organization and the dynamics of the consequence map that was developed. That is the power of consequence maps: system structures are similar across systems, so a consequence map from one system typically works very well in another system.

As mentioned in the opening section of this chapter, this consequence map is only a portion of the entire organizational system for the non-profit. The other side of the organization is service delivery to its clients, and that was not covered. The reader can see that there would obviously be a connection through the variable *Standard Work*, but the consequence seen so far in this chapter is only about a fourth of a total organization consequence map, which, in addition to service delivery, would also include finances and most likely some variables related to the clientele that the non-profit services. However, for the purposes of this project, we were able to isolate the grant proposal writing process and successfully make interventions without the need to widen the scope to include all other organizational variables. Sometimes you get lucky and can keep the consequence map fairly simple to address the immediate problems. I will reiterate what I said at the end of Chapter 4. When building consequence maps, you want just enough scope to adequately cover the situation at hand and all the relevant elements and variables that might play a role. You want to avoid making the consequence maps too large, complicated, and confusing on the first draft. Expand only when necessary to include other elements that might play a part in the feedback loops that are driving the system. Always try to start small, as we did in Figure 5.1. Then, grow and expand the map a little bit at a time, continually checking whether you have all the major feedback loops that impact your system.

Chapter 6

Example Consequence Map for a Management Culture within a Defense Contractor Program

This chapter walks through the specific use of consequence mapping to understand the short-term and long-term consequences of the current "culture" of a specific program for a large defense contractor. For sensitivity purposes, no details can be shared about this specific example. Only generic terms will be used. Similarly to Chapter 5, we will begin with the overall consequence map and then dive into the details of the key feedback loops.

In this example, the key metric of concern that kicked off the analysis effort was the overall program performance. Was it good or bad compared with what the government customer expected? Over the last year, this particular program had suffered a loss in the level of performance and was doing slightly worse than previous levels of performance. The concern for management was that the level of performance, while only slightly worse at this point in time, was trending downward, such that the program performance would most likely deteriorate even more if nothing were done to correct it.

As we dug into some of the reasons why program performance had been poor over the last year, several recurring comments kept coming up. The most commonly listed cause was the "lack of good program performance data." As one employee stated, "If you ask five different people to tell you how the program is doing, you'll get five different answers. Not different interpretations of the same information, but completely different information, which leads to different answers." The second most commonly listed cause was the lack of support from the program analytics group, which was supposed to create reports for all the other groups on the program. A primary role of the program analytics group is to provide each integrated product team (IPT) with charts and reports that indicate how that particular IPT is doing. There were 12 IPTs on this program. With this approach, each IPT leader could then follow up with the program analytics group, as needed, to get more details to find out which lower-level departments or functions participating on the IPT were contributing to the poor performance. The third most commonly listed cause was the lack of supplier performance data. For this particular program, this company was the prime contractor and had several other defense companies as subcontractors that provided either material or labor. These subcontractors made up 50% of the total program, so they contributed a significant amount to the overall performance of the program. The issue was that the performance data provided by the subcontractors was often very delayed (by as much as two or three months) or, if the data was on time, it was incomplete (i.e., data was provided for only a few of the IPTs). Thus, three elements that we wanted to make sure we included in the consequence map were the following:

- Poor program performance data
- Insufficient program analytics reporting capacity
- Poor subcontractor performance data

The Full Consequence Map

The full consequence map is composed of two separate maps that interconnect (Figures 6.1 and 6.2). As with most consequence map exercises, there were multiple versions of the consequence map in Figure 6.1. With each version, some of the elements and connecting arrows were removed, combined, or edited, which helped to refine and clarify the consequence map. The point is that the consequence map shown in Figure 6.1 was the result of many refinements and was not the first consequence map drawn. It is important for the reader to understand that a lot of refinement is often needed, so that the reader does not get the impression that consequence maps are quickly and easily drawn. It is an iterative process. The first map is drawn and communicated. Based on feedback and areas of ambiguity, corrections are made, another map is drawn and communicated, and so on. Thus, as Figures 6.1 and 6.2 are described, keep in mind that a great deal of work went into making sure the words, arrows, and entities did the best possible job of accurately describing the interconnections that existed.

In Figure 6.1, the S/O (same, opposite) terminology is used instead of the +/– (proportional, inversely proportional) for arrow connections. Start with *Program Pressures* in the middle of the top of the graphic. *Program Pressures* come from poor program performance; there is "pressure" to make some changes to improve performance.

(Note: I want to jump ahead a little bit and emphasize that "program performance" itself was not a key metric to include in the consequence map. As the multiple iterations of the consequence map were developed and refined, the discussions about program performance centered more around the accuracy of the performance data for the program. The management of the program were very experienced with programs like this and had been very successful in the past. To them, the degradation of program performance related to a degradation in the quality of the performance data that was available for management to use to make decisions and take corrective actions. If management had accurate information in a timely manner, they had a proven track record of managing the program appropriately to maintain acceptable or exceptional program performance with regard to customer expectations. The reader will see this appear as *Data Integrity* in Figure 6.1, which will be explained in a later paragraph.)

Continuing with Figure 6.1, based on feeling the *Program Pressures*, the program manager (PM) for the overall program then focuses on the metrics for the prime contractor (*Focus on Company Metrics*) and the metrics for the subcontractors (*Focus on Subs Metrics*). The S on the arrows indicates that higher *Program Pressures* lead to more focus. Notice that there is an arrow with an O going from *Focus on Company Metrics* to *Focus on Subs Metrics* to represent that there is limited focus available. When more focus is given to the prime contractor (*Focus on Company*

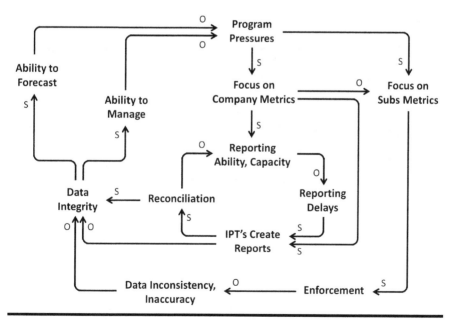

Figure 6.1 Program consequence map.

Metrics), which is the natural tendency of the PM, then less focus can be given to the subcontractors (*Focus on Subs Metrics*). Continuing down the middle of the diagram, *Focus on Company Metrics* has an impact on *Reporting Ability, Capacity* of the program analytics team. The S on the arrow indicates that when *Focus on Company Metrics* is high, there is pressure on the program analytics group to create more reports to track performance, and so on. The *Focus on Company Metrics* also has an S arrow into *IPT's Create Reports*. The higher the *Focus on Company Metrics*, the more pressure the IPTs feel to generate results, which includes the IPTs creating their own performance reports. (This element, *IPT's Create Reports*, will be discussed in more detail in the next paragraph.)

Reporting Ability, Capacity has an impact on *Reporting Delays*, because if there is insufficient capacity in the program analytics group to generate data and reports, it takes the group longer to generate those data and reports. The O shows that these elements move in opposite directions. For example, assume that a typical report takes one full day to complete (with data collection, formatting, and so on). If the program analytics group has five people, then the group has the capacity to generate five reports per day. If 20 reports were needed, this would take the group four days in total (20 reports ÷ 5 reports/day = 4 days). However, if the group has only four people, then the capacity drops to four reports per day, and the same 20 reports now take five days to complete (20 reports ÷ 4 reports/day = 5 days). Consequently, there is a one-day delay. As the delays increase, the IPTs get more impatient and desperate for reports to understand how they are performing. As a result, the IPTs stop waiting for the program analytics group to generate reports, and instead, the IPTs try to generate their own reports (*IPT's Create Reports*). The longer the delays, the more the IPTs put efforts into creating their own reports, because they cannot wait that long to find out how they are doing. Since the IPTs do not have special expertise in generating these performance progress reports (i.e., the skillset of the program analytics group), the IPTs often use incomplete data or educated "guesses" about the data. Again, the skillset for finding the data and generating reports resides within the program analytics group. So, when IPTs try to do it, the IPTs are not getting the full picture or are not using the correct data sets. This leads to the need for *Reconciliation* of the data and reports. In other words, the program analytics team now has to see what the IPTs are generating and compare that with the reports that the program analytics team would create to find out where there are data gaps, data insufficiencies, incorrect data, and so on. Even though the IPTs are trying their best and have the best intentions, it is not their area of expertise, so their work is often incomplete and needs to be fixed to get an accurate assessment of performance for the IPT. This *Reconciliation* effort strips capacity away from the program analytics group (*Reporting Ability, Capacity*), as indicated by the O on the arrowhead.

Also, notice that *Reconciliation* has an impact on the level of *Data Integrity* (correctness, accuracy). The S on the arrowhead indicates that more *Reconciliation* leads to higher *Data Integrity* (and less *Reconciliation* leads to lower *Data Integrity*). That is, the more efforts that are taken to correct the data, reports, and so on, then the better the data is. However, as pointed out in the previous paragraph, the efforts of the IPTs to generate their own reports decrease this *Data Integrity*, because the IPTs do not always use the appropriate data sources and so on. Thus, there is an arrow with an O going from *IPT's Create Reports* to *Data Integrity*.

The accuracy of the program performance data (*Data Integrity*) has an impact on the *Ability to Manage* the program. If *Data Integrity* is low, the *Ability to Manage* the program correctly is low. Incorrect or incomplete data leads to incorrect or incomplete management actions. For example, if the program performance data seems to indicate that the program is ahead of schedule, the PM may decide to shift some resources off the program to save money, because the capacity of these resources is not needed (since they are ahead of schedule and can slow down). If that data is wrong, and, in reality, the program is behind schedule, then the management corrective action of shifting resources off the program will make the situation worse. The program will fall further behind schedule because of a lack of capacity to do the work. The *Ability to Manage* then has a direct impact on the *Program Pressures*. As shown by the O on the arrowhead, if the *Ability to Manage* the program is low (poor), then there is an increase in the *Program Pressures* (because the wrong decisions are being made and making the performance worse). Similar to the *Ability to Manage* is the *Ability to Forecast*. The *Ability to Manage* represents immediate course correction in the near term. The *Ability to Forecast* represents the longer-term ability to show what will or could happen in the future. As such, it is still part of the management process, which impacts program performance (and *Program Pressures*). For example, if the forecast shows that the program will be back on schedule in six months, then the PM may decide not to hire some new people (which takes several months to accomplish). If that forecast is wrong, and, in reality, the program will not be back on schedule until 12–18 months in the future, then the PM has lost the window of opportunity to hire people in time to get the program back on schedule. Defense programs are often many years long, or even decades long, and things tend to move slowly, so forecasting performance and making decisions early enough is very important.

Let us now focus on the right side and bottom of Figure 6.1. On the right side, we have already discussed that *Program Pressures* leads to a *Focus on Subs Metrics*. The level of *Focus on Subs Metrics* is then proportional to the amount of *Enforcement* that the prime contractor levies on the subcontractors (as indicated by the S arrow). So, when *Focus on Subs Metrics* is high, the level of *Enforcement* is high. In this regard, *Enforcement* represents the pressure that the prime contractor puts on the subcontractors to follow the exact formats for submitting data, the exact dates when data is due to the prime contractor, and so on. When *Enforcement* is low, the prime contractor does not care much about the content of the data or when the data is made available to the prime contractor. In these cases, the prime contractor has turned most of its attention to *Focus on Company Metrics* to try to improve its own performance (as opposed to the performance of the subcontractors). As might be expected, when *Enforcement* is low, there is a tendency for *Data Inconsistency, Inaccuracy* to increase (as seen with the O arrow). In other words, if the subcontractors are not held to any specific set of formats or due dates for data delivery, then the data tends to arrive in different formats with different levels of "completeness." It is not that the sky is falling and the data is horrible; there are just minor differences in formatting that do not allow the subcontractor performance data to be easily combined/appended with other data. Or, the data from the subcontractors is later than expected, causing "holes" in the data (i.e., it is incomplete), which makes it impossible to get the full picture of performance. Finally, the level of *Data Inconsistency, Inaccuracy* from the subcontractors has an inversely proportional effect on the overall level of program *Data Integrity*.

In the end, the consequence map in Figure 6.1 has provided a way to interconnect the three most commonly cited problems mentioned in the first section of this chapter:

- Poor program performance data (*Data Integrity*)
- Insufficient program analytics reporting capacity (*Reporting Ability, Capacity*)
- Poor subcontractor performance data (*Data Inconsistency, Inaccuracy*)

Figure 6.1 shows two major impacts on the program *Data Integrity*: from *Reconciliation* (on the side of the prime contractor) and *Data Inconsistency, Inaccuracy* (on the side of the subcontractors). Within the prime contractor, *Reconciliation* is driven, in part, by the lack of *Reporting Ability, Capacity* that causes impatient IPTs to create their own reports, which are often incomplete and insufficient compared with the more thorough analysis provided by the program analytics group.

This first consequence map provided a lot of insight for the prime contractor organization with regard to why the program was having some issues. The PM and IPTs could see how they contributed directly to the issue through the proliferation of additional IPT reports, as well as how they contributed indirectly to the issue through their management (or lack of management) of the subcontractors. In total, the PM and IPTs could see how the evolving management culture was playing a major role in the degradation of program performance.

However, at this point, the question was asked, "What else contributes to the program data issue?" In the discussions, the most common cause was the delay between receiving authorization to do some work on the program and the negotiation and subsequent funding of that work. Figure 6.2 shows how this was incorporated and connected to the consequence map of Figure 6.1. In Figure 6.2, *Program Pressures* cause an additional *Desire to Make Progress* to get the program back on track (S on the arrow). The program is behind, so we need to do more. This was experienced at both the prime contractor organization and the customer organization (which is external to the prime contractor). The higher the *Program Pressures* (due to poor performance), the higher the *Desire to Make Progress*. One of the ways to make more progress is for the customer organization to *Authorize Work*, which

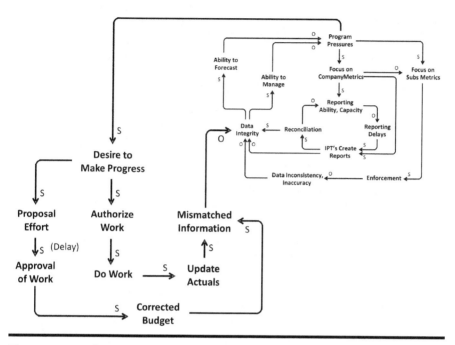

Figure 6.2   Entire system consequence map.

then allows the prime contractor (and subcontractors) to *Do Work* (S on the arrow). In this case, the "work" is above and beyond the originally contracted work or is a significant change to the originally contracted work. It is very common on large defense contracts for the program to grow in terms of work (or for some of the work content to change significantly). Since these programs are large, last for several years, and often involve the development of new technology (which introduces a great deal of uncertainty), it is very common for the scope of the program to change or grow over time through additional work. After the work is done (*Do Work*), the actual costs for the work are captured in the accounting system for the program (*Update Actuals*).

In theory, for any additional work (or significant change in current work content) on a program, a request would be sent by the government customer, and the prime contractor would submit a proposal in response to that request. Once a proposal was submitted, the government and the prime contractor would negotiate back and forth until a final amount was agreed on. Depending on the work, this proposal may involve work from subcontractors, which means that the prime contractor needs to collect proposals from all the subcontractors (after negotiating with them) to then put together the full proposal for the additional work requested by the government customer. At this point in time, the government customer would issue an authorization to proceed with the work, and every party involved would know exactly what was expected of them and for what price. To accelerate this process, it is an accepted practice on many defense programs for work to be authorized to proceed without a final negotiated contract in place. Of course, this approach has some risk, because each party is signing up for something that is not completely defined, but the approach has the benefit of moving work along quickly. On the bottom left of Figure 6.2, the proposal process follows in parallel with the work process. Just as the *Desire to Make Progress* leads to *Authorize Work*, the *Desire to Make Progress* also leads to *Proposal Efforts*. After a significant delay, the proposal is negotiated and leads to the formal *Approval of Work*. Based on the final negotiated contract, the budget for the program is corrected to match these negotiated costs and prices (in *Corrected Budget*).

The actual costs of doing the work (*Update Actuals*) and the final negotiated costs for the work (*Corrected Budget*) come together in *Mismatched Information*. The term *Mismatched Information* is used because there is often a long delay between when the negotiated costs and the actual costs for that same work are input into the financial system. The financial system captures all types of information to provide performance data. In this case, for a particular piece of additional work, what did it cost to do that work compared with the negotiated cost? In many instances, the work is complete even before a negotiated cost is finalized. At that point in time, how can the program tell how it is doing? Therefore, we used the term *Mismatched Information* to signify that these two values are rarely in the financial system at the same time. The S arrows indicate that more authorized work and more proposal work contribute to *Mismatched Information*, because they are out of synch. As a result, managers have to guess or estimate what the final negotiated cost will be to enable them to make a comparison against actuals to determine the current performance level for the program. Later, when the negotiated costs for the pre-authorized work are input into the system, the performance level can look completely different. Finally, the *Mismatched Information* impacts the *Data Integrity*. The O on the arrow indicates that when the amount of *Mismatched Information* is high, the *Data Integrity* is low.

The Feedback Loops

There are many feedback loops in the overall consequence map, but we are going to focus on the four major feedback loops that tend to drive behavior for this program. These four feedback loops represent dynamics at the IPT level, the prime contractor level, the program level (with subcontractors), and the customer level (Figures 6.3 through 6.6, respectively).

Figure 6.3 shows the positive (reinforcing) feedback loop that operates at the level of the IPTs (even number of Os in the loop). In this loop, insufficient capacity in the program analytics group causes delays in reporting. The delays are too long for IPTs to take meaningful management corrective actions, so the IPTs create their own reports. Eventually, these reports have to be reconciled with the "official"

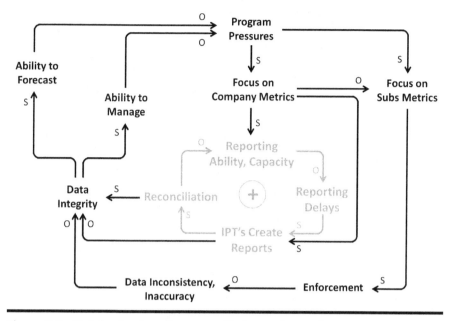

Figure 6.3   Reinforcing loop for reconciliation and capacity.

reports of the program analytics group. This reconciliation work (i.e., rework) strips capacity away from doing the "normal" work of the program analytics group, which causes more delays in reporting, and the loop continues. Moreover, the high level of *Reconciliation* work contributes to low *Data Integrity*, which has its own terrible consequences.

As with other example consequence maps shown in Chapters 4 and 5, this positive (reinforcing) feedback loop is operating in the opposite direction to the desired performance, so it is a vicious loop. However, as with all positive feedback loops, if the "direction" of the loop dynamics can be changed, the structure still drives behavior in the same direction, so there is the possibility of a virtuous loop. With the virtuous loop, sufficient capacity would exist in the program analytics group that reporting could be done quickly, and IPTs would be able to use the reports from the program analytics group to manage their IPTs in a timely manner. There would be very few, if any, reports generated by the IPTs and therefore, less reconciliation work (or ideally, no reconciliation work). Less *Reconciliation* leads to higher *Data Integrity*.

Figure 6.4 shows the positive (reinforcing) feedback loop that operates at the level of the prime contractor (even number of Os in the loop). *Program Pressures* from poor performance cause the PM of the prime contractor to lean toward focusing on their own performance metrics to improve the overall program performance (as opposed to the subcontractors). This PM focus results in greater IPT management focus and pressure on the IPTs to improve performance. Thus, the IPTs generate

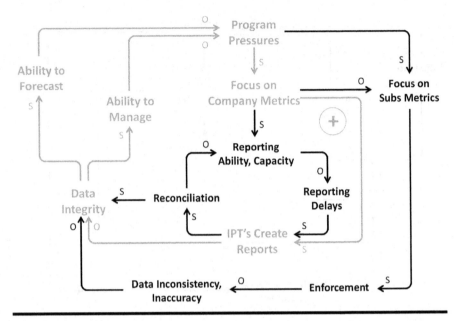

Figure 6.4 Reinforcing loop for Data Integrity and company focus.

more of their own reports in an attempt to get information more quickly, which decreases the performance *Data Integrity*. With poor *Data Integrity*, it becomes difficult for the PM to manage and forecast effectively, which only increases the *Program Pressures*. As with all positive (reinforcing) feedback loops, this structure can work in a favorable fashion. If *Data Integrity* is high, management and forecasts become more effective and appropriate, which decreases *Program Pressures* and the proliferation of IPT-generated reports. Fewer IPT-generated reports lead to higher *Data Integrity*, and so on.

Figure 6.5 shows the negative (balancing) feedback loop that operates at the level of the program (odd number of Os in the loop), which includes subcontractors. Similarly to the feedback loop in Figure 6.4, this loop operates through the subcontractors and also impacts *Data Integrity*. However, this loop operates to improve the *Data Integrity* by enforcing strict performance data requirements with the subcontractors. As a negative (balancing) feedback loop, this loop essentially causes a focus on the subcontractors based on the level of *Program Pressures*. Somewhat like a thermostat in a room that heats or cools the room based on a desired temperature, this loop drives enforcement on the subcontractors based on an "acceptable" level of *Program Pressures*. For example, the PM can handle a certain amount of pressure. Nothing goes perfectly, so it is expected that there will be some bumps along the way. As long as the *Program Pressures* are below that level, there is no need to panic and push the subcontractors, because "all is well." But beyond that level of pressure, the PM needs to respond by pushing requirements on

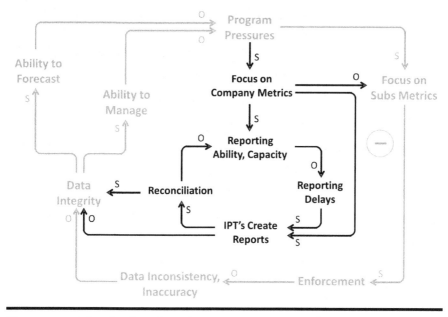

Figure 6.5   Balancing loop for subcontractor Data Integrity.

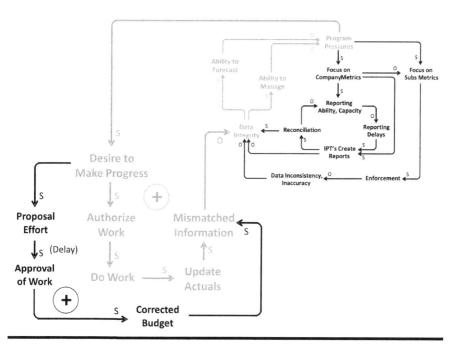

Figure 6.6   Customer-driven reinforcing loops.

the subcontractors to improve the *Data Integrity* to get the *Program Pressures* back to the "acceptable" level.

Figure 6.6 shows the positive (reinforcing) feedback loop that operates at the level of the government customer (even number of Os in the loop). The figure actually shows two positive feedback loops, but they work in parallel and contribute to the same overall feedback loop, so only the feedback loop highlighted in gray will be discussed. This gray positive (reinforcing) feedback loop primarily shows that the *Desire to Make Progress* (due to high *Program Pressures*) creates more *Mismatched Information*, which drives *Data Integrity* down, which in turn, increases the *Program Pressures*. What makes this feedback loop so important is that it is primarily driven by the government customer. That is, the customer sees poor performance and desires more work to get done, so the customer is often the one that pushes work to be authorized (without negotiating and completing the proposal). In an attempt to respond to the customer, it is very difficult for the prime contractor to say "no" in this situation. But, that's another story … with its own consequence map.

What Does the Consequence Map Show Us?

To summarize the figures in the previous section, there are four main feedback loops of concern:

- Positive (reinforcing) loop at the IPT level, in which insufficient reporting capacity leads to other reports and reconciliation
- Positive (reinforcing) loop at the prime contractor level, in which management pressure encourages other reports and reconciliation
- Negative (balancing) loop at the program level, in which the prime contractor enforces data requirements based on the level of pressure experienced by the program
- Positive (reinforcing) loop at the customer level, in which the customer's desire to move ahead on authorized work adds to the Data Integrity issue

These feedback loops directly affect the original issue of poor program performance arising from inaccurate and incomplete performance data (which is used by management to determine what actions should be taken on the program to keep it on schedule and on budget). In fact, except for the IPT-level feedback loop, all of these feedback loops have *Data Integrity* as an element within the feedback loop. And, the IPT-level feedback loop has *Data Integrity* as an element that is impacted by the feedback loop (through *Reconciliation*). This is important, because it means that there may be many opportunities to improve the accuracy and completeness of the program performance data (which will lead to better management actions and better program performance). It is also easy to see why there are data issues.

With consequence maps, issues are de-politicized. In this particular defense organization, some other, higher-priority programs caused the initial decrease in program analytics capacity. Corporate management made the decision to dedicate some key people from the program analytics group (which supported all programs as a corporate-wide function) to another large program within the company. At the beginning of the program, this was not the case, which is why performance was good in the beginning. It took some time for this reduction in program analytics capacity to play out enough to have an impact. When IPTs found themselves fighting for the time of the program analytics resources and felt as if they were "competing" with other IPTs to create their own reports, it was obvious that something had to be done. By that point, there was some animosity among the IPTs, which also spread to the customer. As with many issues in many organizations, the behaviors of people involved were not ideal, and there was a good amount of finger-pointing and blame. Creating the consequence map allowed all parties involved in the program (prime contractor, subcontractors, and customer) to see the sources of their issues. The system structure was causing the behavior. Now that everyone could see the system structure, the blaming stopped, and there was movement toward solutions.

Also, with consequence maps, solutions become very obvious to all participants. Perhaps we cannot directly change some of the elements, but there will typically be at least one element in a feedback loop that can act as an intervention point over which management has some control and authority. However, even if some elements cannot be directly changed through the formal introduction of a new policy and so on, everyone is aware of the interconnecting feedback loops and the dynamics they produce, which often eases tensions and allows "indirect" changes to some elements. For example, in this particular defense case, when management feel *Program Pressures*, they can decide not to act as swiftly and harshly as before. Instead, management can realize that the pressure they pass on to other parts of the organization has an impact, so if management apply less pressure on other parts of the organization, the strength of the feedback loop can be reduced. The feedback loop is not eliminated or switched in the opposite direction, but at least, the feedback loop is not as dominant as before.

Figure 6.7 introduces two easy opportunities for intervention points in this defense program management system:

■ Additional *Reporting Ability, Capacity* can be added by either hiring new resources, shifting priorities at the corporate level to re-assign resources back to this program, or hiring outside contractors to fill the role.
■ Strict *Enforcement* can be maintained for the subcontractors, so that the data coming from subcontractors is consistently complete and timely and thus, is not a contributor to the deterioration of *Data Integrity*.

For this particular organization, a combination of two options was implemented to add capacity to the program analytics group. First, the PM of the program (after

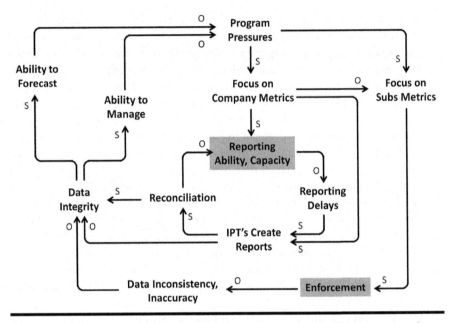

Figure 6.7 Opportunities for intervention at company level (Figure 6.8 shows additional opportunities for intervention at the customer level).

realizing the impact that this lack of capacity was having on the program) decided to use management reserve to cover the cost of hiring a few additional resources full-time. The program still had three years remaining, so there was plenty of business justification for bringing on new resources. It took approximately four months to get these resources on board and trained. So, in the near term, the PM of the program decided to use management reserve funds to cover the cost of a team of external contractors to come in and fill the gap. After about six months, the program could see a difference in the consistency of the data used for performance management. There were still some issues, but it was clear that the trend was moving in the right direction and that better performance data was available with much shorter delays.

For enforcement of the data inputs from the subcontractors, a little more work had to be done. One of the issues for this program was that each major subcontractor (of which there were five) had its own "point of contact" in the prime contractor. Essentially, a person was assigned to coordinate with each subcontractor. Each person had his or her own idea on what the data should look like, and so on, so there ended up being five different formats and schedules for data inputs from all subcontractors. There was a little bit of overlap among some of the expectations for different subcontractors, but mostly, they were different. Consequently, the first change to make was to get a consistent format and schedule that all five points of contact and all five subcontractors could agree to. This took approximately three months of meetings, flowcharts, and negotiations. However, in the end, a single format and schedule were developed and agreed on. It took another three months for all points of contact and all subcontractors to make the necessary internal changes and get used to the new format and schedule. This improvement helped tremendously. With the same format and schedule in place, enforcement of data inputs was much easier. It still required some discipline on the part of the prime contractor points of contact for them to "push" their subcontractors when they did not follow the format or schedule, but eventually all the points of contact got comfortable with it, along with all the subcontractors. After another few months of this new approach, all the kinks were ironed out, and there were no more data issues with subcontractors. The original issues were completely eliminated. These changes at the subcontractor level, combined with the additional capacity for program analytics, helped improve *Data Integrity* significantly, which gave the PM a more accurate status of the program, so that the correct management actions could be taken. Program performance was not trending upward.

Decrease the *Desire to Make Progress* so that there is not a push to *Authorize Work* at such a fast pace.

Typically, in the defense environment, a defense company will take whatever work the government customer wants to give it. This is not true in all cases, but usually, the defense company will find a way to accept the work (or at least, accept the prime contractor role and farm out work to subcontractors).

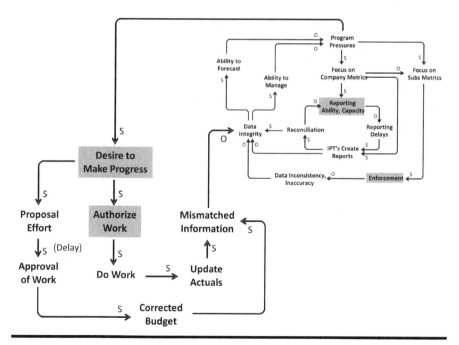

Figure 6.8 Opportunities for intervention with customer.

Therefore, it is very odd for a company to turn down work or try to delay the work. Therefore, when the prime contractor made this request to the government customer, the customer was quite surprised. After the consequence map had been shared with the customer, the customer immediately saw the part that it played in making the situation worse. In a sense, everyone sort of "knew" that the disconnect between the authorization of the work and the negotiation of the proposal was not ideal, but it had never been captured like this in a consequence map that showed where and how the disconnect caused problems in other parts of the system. The customer was quite willing to slow down the additional work authorizations so that they aligned better with the timing of the proposals. The timing is not perfect yet. That is, much of the work moves along ahead of the proposal, but the delay between the two has been reduced, so that the disparity is not as large as before (which helps make the financial data more accurate). Both the customer and the prime contractor realize that this may never completely go away. Sometimes, there are new capabilities that need to be added because of new technologies or inventions that did not exist when the program started. However, both sides realize the impact that this has, so both sides now work diligently to reduce the delays and increase communication between those doing the work and those doing the proposals.

Final Remarks

In this defense example, the four feedback loops represent "layers" of the problem, like layers of an onion (Figure 6.9). The innermost layer (the first layer) is very local to the IPTs. The next outer layer (the second layer) is at the prime contractor company level. The next outer layer (the third layer) is at the program level (which involves the subcontractors). The final layer (the fourth layer) is at the customer level. Of course, this could be expanded into multiple layers. For example, at the

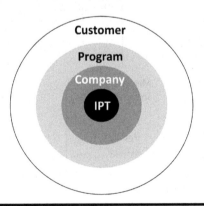

Figure 6.9   Multiple layers of consequence mapping.

company layer, this was only one program within a portfolio of programs for the prime contractor. As discussed in the previous section of this chapter, the corporate decision to shift program analytics resources had an impact. A larger consequence map could be made that shows how all programs and all resources within the entire defense company interconnect. As another example, this program is also just one in a portfolio for the government customer. A similar expansion of the consequence map at the customer level could show the interconnections with other programs, and so on.

However, the goal of a consequence mapping exercise is not to capture the whole world. The goal is to capture the feedback loops that drive the dynamics, behaviors, or issues that are experienced by the organization or system. The consequence maps in Figures 6.1 and 6.2 accomplished this. With the implementation of a couple of changes at the prime contractor (adding reporting capacity, enforcing a common format and schedule with subcontractors) and discussions with the government customer on the difficulties that the work acceleration caused, the quality and timeliness of the performance data for the program improved, which allowed management to make more appropriate decisions on what actions to take. Any reader involved in the defense industry can probably relate to the issues described in this chapter and agree with some of the interventions. Hopefully, the consequence maps have provided a few insights that the reader can take back to his or her organization.

SYSTEM DYNAMICS SIMULATION

3

Chapter 7

Simulation Using System Dynamics

Disclaimer: This chapter is not intended to be a thorough description or training in system dynamics (SD), a type of continuous simulation approach. This chapter could barely be considered a basic primer. The purpose of this chapter is to explain enough about SD to enable the reader to understand the discussions in Chapters 8 and 9. References at the end of this chapter are much better resources for the reader who wants to learn more about SD. Chapters 8 and 9 walk through the translation of consequence maps into simulation models for the purpose of quantifying the values to guide management with detailed decision making.

> People would never attempt to send a space ship to the moon without first testing the equipment by constructing prototype models and by computer simulation .... Our social systems are far more complex and harder to understand than our technological systems. Why, then, do we not use the same approach of making models of social systems and conducting laboratory experiments on those models before we try new laws and government programs in real life? The stated answer is often that our knowledge of social systems is insufficient for constructing useful models. But what justification can there be for the apparent assumption that we do not know enough to construct models but believe we do know enough to design new social systems directly by passing laws and starting new social programs?
>
> *Collected Papers of Jay W. Forrester, 1975, pp. 212–213*

Statistical Modeling and Structure Modeling

Everything is a process. Any action taken in an organization, any decision made, or any system operated represents a process. For any process, there are inputs, some activities occur, and some results are provided. The activities of the process provide a transformation of the inputs into some output or result that is different from the original state of the inputs (Figure 7.1). Of course, this is a very simple view of a process. There are books full of more complete descriptions. But, it will suffice for the following discussion.

The purpose of using this simple view of a process is to illustrate how SD differs from typical modeling approaches used in businesses and organizations. The typical approach is a *statistical* approach. With the statistical approach, the model is built entirely on data about the process. The process itself (i.e., the Activities in Figure 7.1) is considered a black box. The assumption is that we can know everything about the process and its activities by analyzing its output results. For example, imagine the following process:

- When the input is 1, the output is 2.
- When the input is 2, the output is 4.
- When the input is 3, the output is 6.

With this information about the process, it is easy to assume that the process multiplies the input by a factor of two. If we were to graph the output, it would be a

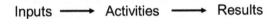

Inputs ⟶ Activities ⟶ Results

Figure 7.1 Activities (processes) require inputs and produce results (outputs).

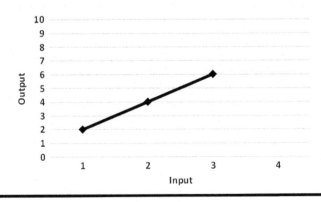

Figure 7.2 Simple example of inputs and output.

straight line. Figure 7.2 shows a graph of the process inputs (horizontal axis) and outputs (vertical axis). Generally, we would say that we could use that straight line to project what the future results of the process might be. For instance, the line would show that the next output in the "pattern" would be 8 (i.e., 2, 4, 6, 8), as shown in Figure 7.3 with the dashed gray line. This is a common approach to forecasting sales for an organization. What have sales looked like over the past few months or years? Okay, we will assume that pattern will continue, and we will forecast the next several months' sales based on continuing to draw the "line" into the future. As shown in Figure 7.4, statistical modeling attempts to project future results by extrapolating historical data from the process. This extrapolation may end up with a straight line (as in Figure 7.3) or a curve of some sort. The line or curve is typically called a *trend*, and it shows the most likely output of the process given all the data we have from the history of the process (i.e., data from the past).

While this is a commonly used approach, and there is a quite a bit of science surrounding this approach, the statistical approach suffers from several weaknesses. In fact, it should be noted that every approach to analyzing data or processes has some weaknesses and some strengths. For the statistical approach, its strengths are the following:

■ It is fairly simple to use (even though the math behind it may be very complex).
■ It typically can be done in a spreadsheet (which is a very popular and ubiquitous tool for organizations).
■ It is relatively accurate for short-term projections (because not much usually changes in the short term, so the "momentum" of the process keeps the results following a similar pattern for the short term).

However, its first weakness is that the statistical approach is *extremely* dependent on the "quality" of the data used. Often, the people doing the data analysis will say they have to "scrub the data" or "remove the outliers." They do this because the

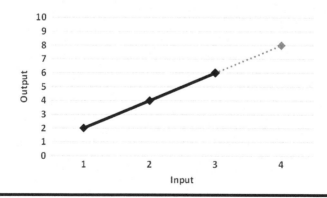

Figure 7.3   Simple example of forecasting future results with a trend line.

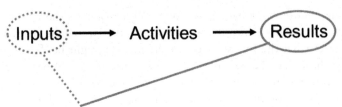

- **Statistical** modeling attempts to project future results by extrapolating historical process data into trends:
  - Highly dependent on the quality of data used to generate trends
  - Focuses on results (sometimes using correlations with inputs), with no consideration for the activities
  - Does not project well when future is significantly different from past

Figure 7.4   Statistical modeling looks at data about the activities.

quality of the data is not as high as desired. Because the statistical approach only uses data, this data must be perfect (or almost perfect) to create a trend curve in which the analyst has high confidence. If there is not enough data, a good statistical model cannot be created. So, for this approach, a lot of high-quality data is needed. This is often not the case in many organizations, which limits the usefulness of the approach.

Second, the statistical approach typically just focuses on output data (results). This is data *after* the process has occurred. There is no consideration of the activities within the process itself. The process is treated as a black box that is not opened. In Figure 7.4, the solid line around Results signifies this. In some cases, Inputs are strongly correlated to Results, so that Inputs can become leading indicators of the output Results. Consider the simple example again:

- When the input is 1, the output is 2.
- When the input is 2, the output is 4.
- When the input is 3, the output is 6.

As portrayed earlier in Figures 7.2 and 7.3, the typical approach is to look at the output data (2, 4, 6) and create a trend for the expected output results (2, 4, 6, 8). In this simple example, there is a strong correlation between the inputs and outputs. In fact, it is a perfect correlation. So, it would be easy to look at the inputs (1, 2, 3) and say that the next input will be 4, which will provide an output of 8. This method is not always used, so there is a dotted line around Inputs in Figure 7.4.

In the previous paragraph, the statement was made that the statistical approach does not consider the process activities. For instance, in this simple example, it *looks* as if the process is multiplying the input by a factor of two:

$$y = 2 \times x$$

$$\text{Output} = 2 \times \text{Input}$$

But in reality, the process could be doing something much more complex. For example, it could be the following, which yields the same results:

$$y = \left[2 \times \left(x^2 - 1 \right) \big/ \left(x - 1 \right) \right] - 2$$

$$\text{Output} = \left[2 \times \left(\text{Input}^2 - 1 \right) \big/ \left(\text{Input} - 1 \right) \right] - 2$$

We do not know. And with the statistical approach, we do not really care. If we have data that consistently shows a pattern, we will assume that pattern is good, and we will use it to forecast into the future.

Third, and most importantly, the statistical approach loses its strength and validity when the future conditions are not similar to the historical conditions. Since the approach uses data from the past, it logically follows that the projections and forecasts from a statistical model are only valid if the conditions in the future match the conditions when the data was collected (in the past). For example, a sales forecast that shows a straight line increasing into the future makes sense when the market for the product remains exactly the same (e.g., same competitors, same products, same prices). If, however, competitors dropped out of the market, new products entered the market, the price of raw materials used to make the product doubled in price, and so on, then the sales forecast would most likely not hold for long. Perhaps in the month immediately following, the sales forecast may be close. It takes a little bit of time for consumers to adjust to new players in the market or for the higher price of raw materials to manifest itself in the final price to the consumers. But, the following months will begin to show very different results, which most likely diverge from the original forecast. Updated forecasts will need to be done every month until enough data is available to create a new, statistically valid model of the "new market."

In contrast to the statistical modeling approach, the *structural* modeling approach focuses on the activities that occur within a process (i.e., actions, decisions). The approach focuses on the system structure; hence the name (Figure 7.5). In fact, in a diametrically opposite way to the statistical approach, the structural approach does not care about the data related to the process for building the model itself. The process data may be used to calibrate or tailor the structural model, but the model is *not dependent* on data to make projections about the process. With the statistical approach, if there is no data, there is no model. Not so with the structural approach. The activities themselves are modeled, and it is the activities that generate output results. In our simple example, this is like knowing the *exact* equation that is used, not just that it *looks* as if the input is multiplied by two.

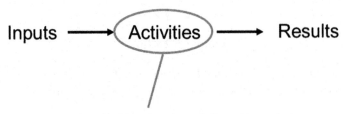

- **Structural** modeling attempts to project future results by simulating the activities or operations:
  - Does not depend on data to create the model because the flow of activities is independent of data
  - Data is used to tailor and calibrate the model (as inputs)
  - Focuses on activities, which generate results

Figure 7.5   Structural modeling looks at the activities.

To repeat, the structural modeling approach does not focus on data but instead, focuses on the process activities themselves. Consequently, an operational or activity-based model is developed that captures all relevant causal relationships (i.e., cause-and-effect relationships) among the various parts or elements of the process (which have been diagramed in a consequence map). Data is still used, but it is now used to calibrate the model and make it unique to a particular process or a particular situation. By incorporating the actual activities into the model, structural forecasting more accurately represents a process and how it will perform. Furthermore, the impacts of management decisions and policies can be incorporated. This allows a structural model to capture changes in the underlying conditions surrounding the process, which is impossible with the statistical approach. As such, the structural approach creates much more realistic and accurate forecasts, especially when future conditions are expected to be different from past conditions, because the activities themselves are simulated. Specifically, the structural approach addresses four major flaws of the statistical approach:

- *Processes are not treated like black boxes.* Process activities are known and modeled. They are not hidden; instead, they form the foundation of the structural model.
- *Models do not depend heavily on historical data.* The structural model, by definition, is independent of process data. It is a model of activities and relationships. Data is used to refine the structural model, but data does not drive the development of a structural model. As a result, even if there is very little process data, a structural model can still be developed and can still be quite effective.

■ *Future conditions can be different from past conditions.* Because the process activities are modeled and are no longer a black box, different conditions can be captured as part of the model. This allows the planner or analyst a wide range of scenario exploration when conducting analyses.

■ *Management decisions and policies are captured.* These are a key part of the structure that defines the system being studied, so they are included in the structural model. Statistical models do not incorporate these management reactions when conditions change.

Without structural simulation, we only understand parts of the system but not the total dynamics of all interactions. Hence, it is impossible to know the true consequences that decisions, policies, and actions will have in the short term and the long term. Without an understanding of true consequences, our best intentions often lead to extremely poor results, because the overall behavior of complex systems is

Year	Calendar Year	Actual Data	Linear Trend	Polynomial Trend
1	1990	300	290	299
2	1991	305	298	301
3	1992	290	306	305
4	1993	301	314	311
5	1994	350	322	318
6	1995	330	331	326
7	1996	337	339	335
8	1997	325	347	344
9	1998	345	355	354
10	1999	360	363	364
11	2000	380	371	373
12	2001	385	379	382
13	2002	404	388	390
14	2003	391	396	398
15	2004	400	404	403
16	2005		412	407
17	2006		420	410
18	2007		428	410
19	2008		436	407
20	2009		445	402
21	2010		453	394
22	2011		461	383
23	2012		469	368
24	2013		477	350
25	2014		485	327

Figure 7.6   Data tables for Figure 7.7.

counterintuitive, and we typically implement changes where they have the least leverage or probability of success.

Figures 7.6 and 7.7 provide a good example of the issues with statistical modeling. Figure 7.6 provides a table of data. The first column from the left is the year (Year 1, Year 2, etc.), and the second column is the calendar year (1990, 1991, etc.). The third column has the output data from an example process. Notice that the process data only goes through 2004 (Year 15). This process data will be used to forecast the next 10 years to 2014 (Year 25). The fourth column, called Linear Trend, provides a best-fit curve for the data from Years 1 to 15 using a straight line. The fifth column, called Polynomial Trend, uses another type of best-fit curve. The key point is that these are two very different trend equations.

Figure 7.7 shows the process data (squares) along with the Linear Trend (straight line) and Polynomial Trend (curved line). The equations for these trends are shown in the graph also. Under each equation is a value for R^2, called the *coefficient of determination*, which is a measure for how well the trend line/curve fits the historical data. If $R^2 = 1$, the trend line/curve fits the data perfectly (i.e., the trend line/curve passes through every single historical data point). As R^2 drops below 1.0, it indicates that the trend line/curve does not fit the historical data very well. In this example, the R^2 value for the Linear Trend is 0.8875, and the R^2 value for the Polynomial Trend is 0.8969; both of these are close to 1.0, which means that they are both good fits. In fact, if we wanted to get very technical, we could say that the Polynomial Trend is a better fit, because it has a slightly higher R^2 value. However,

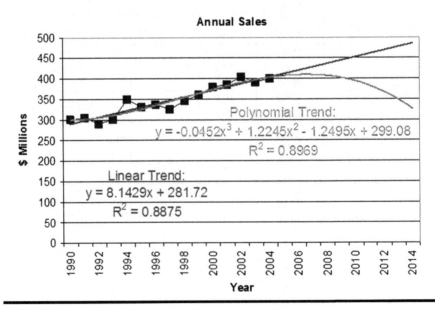

Figure 7.7   Chart for data in Figure 7.6.

in a real-world situation, a manager in an organization would most likely pick the Linear Trend as the forecast for the organization, because it looks more appropriate.

This example serves to point out two things. First, the example shows that even within the statistical approach, there can be vastly different answers. Which answer is most appropriate often ends up being a guessing game. In this example, both trends fit the data equally well, so it is a coin toss as to which one to use as the forecast. Second, the example shows that in the very short term, there is not a significant difference in the two trends. For instance, look at the values in Table 7.6 for Year 16. The Linear Trend predicts 412, and the Polynomial Trend predicts 407. The difference between these two values is 1.2%. For Year 17, the Linear Trend predicts 420, and the Polynomial Trend predicts 410, a difference of 2.4%. However, by Year 25, the Linear Trend predicts 485, and the Polynomial Trend predicts 327, a difference of 33% (if 427 is used as the basis for comparison) or 48% (if 327 is used as the basis of comparison). That is a huge variation from the 1% and 2% difference in the short term. No matter which equation is used, the statistical model will always show similar values in the near term, because the "system" will not change much in the short timeframe. For this reason, the statistical approach continues to be used by organizations. Each year, adjustments are made, and a new forecast is created, which, of course, will look pretty close for the next time period but not for the long term, and the re-forecasting initiative repeats itself.

Overview of System Dynamics Modeling and Simulation Methodology

Figure 1.5 from the book is repeated here as Figure 7.8 as a reminder that system structure generates the behaviors that are seen over time for a system, and these behaviors create the individual output results that are measured for each time period.

SD, invented by Dr. Jay Forrester at MIT in the late 1950s, is a modeling and simulation technique based on engineering control theory that captures the cause-and-effect feedback relationships (i.e., the structure) that exist in complex social, managerial, and operational systems. The approach has been used extensively in all types of organizations because of its realistic and applicable approach for representing service processes, production processes, supply chain interactions, operational activities, and so on. SD models capture the key structural relationships that define the system. The structure, in turn, produces the dynamic behavior shown by the system. The resulting SD simulation mirrors reality, because the underlying model structure includes the appropriate feedback loops, causality, delays, and other relationships.

A good supply chain example of this is the Beer Game, a role-playing game based on the production-distribution model that was the foundation for Forrester's

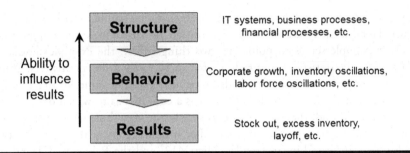

Figure 7.8   Examples of structure, behavior, and results.

seminal book *Industrial Dynamics* (Productivity Press, 1961). The Beer Game was developed to introduce students, managers, and executives to concepts of SD. The purpose of the game is to illustrate the key principle that *system structure produces system behavior.* Players experience the pressures of playing a role in a complex system and can see long-range effects during the course of the game. Each player participates as a member of a team that must meet its customers' demands. The object of the game is to minimize the total cost for your team. Each team consists of a retailer (that sells to the end customer), a distributor, a wholesaler, and a factory (that produces the beer) (Figure 7.9).

In the end, all teams tend to perform basically the same. There is a bump in customer orders to the retailer (e.g., increase from 100 cases of beer per day to 110 cases of beer per day). Then, there are oscillations in inventory at every step of the supply chain, and these oscillations amplify as they move further down into the supply chain, much like the well-known bullwhip effect encountered in many supply chains. The inventory oscillations are minimal at the retailer (the first tier of the supply chain), but they grow enormously as they move through the distributor, the wholesaler, and finally, the factory (the last tier in the supply chain) (Figure 7.10). The reason why this game is such a good example of how structure drives the behavior of a system is because all teams experience the same basic results, regardless of whether the team is composed of seasoned CEOs or high school students. The structure guides the behavior of the system, regardless of who the "employees" are. Even with the best intentions of all the players, the system still thwarts everyone's efforts to succeed. No team ever achieves the low-cost solution.

To help the reader gain better insight into how SD works, a bathtub analogy will be used. With a bathtub, the only way to change the level of water is by opening the faucet to add water and opening the drain to remove water (Figure 7.11).

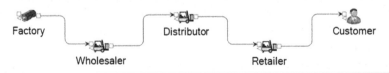

Figure 7.9   Beer Game supply chain.

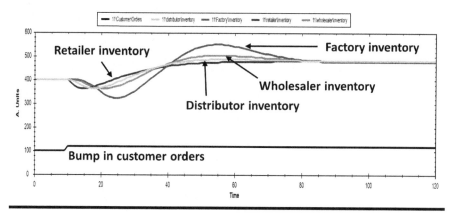

Figure 7.10   Typical Beer Game results.

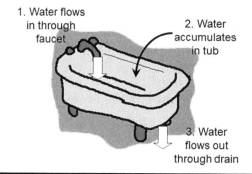

Figure 7.11   Bathtub analogy.

We cannot snap our fingers and immediately have a specific level of water in the tub. As a result, it may take some time to get the water to the desired level, because we have to continue to add or remove water. In a similar manner, the *Cash Balance* (i.e., available money) for an organization is determined by how much money flows into the organization through its *Revenue* stream and how much money exits the organization based on *Expenses* (Figure 7.12). In Figure 7.12, arrows on the flows called *Revenue* and *Expenses* indicate the direction of the flow of money (either into or out of the "bathtub" called *Cash Balance*).

In SD terminology, the level of water in a bathtub or the *Cash Balance* is a called a *stock* or a *level*. A stock or level accumulates things (e.g., water, money), and it is often represented graphically by a box, as in Figure 7.12 for *Cash Balance*. A stock can have *flows* or *rates* coming into and out of the stock that add or remove things from the stock, respectively. Stocks and flows (or levels and rates) are the two fundamental building blocks in SD models. For example, in Figure 7.12, the flow called *Revenue* adds money to the stock *Cash Balance*, and the flow called *Expenses* removes money from the stock *Cash Balance*. For any time period of the simulation,

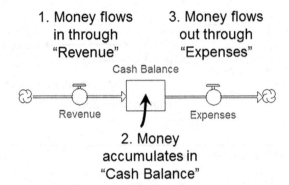

Figure 7.12 **Simple system dynamics model for cash balance.**

the amount of money in the stock *Cash Balance* is equal to the amount of money in the *Cash Balance* from the previous time period plus any *Revenue* (flows into the stock) and minus any *Expenses* (flows out of the stock).

Suppose the *Cash Balance* is $10 million in Year 1, and in Year 2 the *Revenue* is $5 million and the *Expenses* are $3 million. The *Cash Balance* at the end of Year 2 would be $12 million, as follows:

Cash Balance (Year 2) = Cash Balance (Year 1) + Revenue (Year 2) − Expenses (Year 2)

Cash Balance (Year 2)=$10 million+$5 million − $3 million = $12 million

We will now build a slightly more complex example to show how SD captures feedback loops. In Figure 7.13, the simple *Cash Balance* model is expanded to include two other key stocks within an organization: *Personnel* and *Work To Do*. The stock *Personnel* is the accumulation (or number) of employees in the

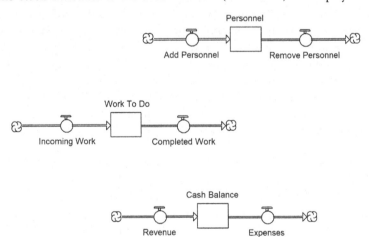

Figure 7.13 **Simple system dynamics model for a company.**

organization. The flow *Add Personnel* (e.g., hiring employees) puts more employees in the stock *Personnel*, and the flow *Remove Personnel* (e.g., firing employees) takes employees out of the stock *Personnel*. In a similar fashion, *Work To Do* is the accumulation of work that the organization has to accomplish (e.g., service orders from customers). The flow *Incoming Work* (e.g., new customer orders) puts more work in the stock *Work To Do*, and the flow *Completed Work* (e.g., fulfilled orders) takes work out of the stock *Work To Do*.

In Figure 7.14, additional circles (other than flows), such as *Customer Demand*, capture other variables and/or equations needed to calculate flows. The smaller, thin arrows indicate connections between variables. Multiple interconnections can create feedback loops. Figure 7.14 shows a negative, balancing feedback loop that represents management adjustments to adding *Personnel* at a company based on available money. Starting at the top of the diagram with *Personnel*, the number of *Personnel* available determines how much work can be completed. The amount of *Completed Work*, when multiplied by a *Price per Unit*, then determines how much *Revenue* is generated for the company. At the same time, the number of *Personnel*, when multiplied by an *Average Salary*, determines the *Expenses* for the company

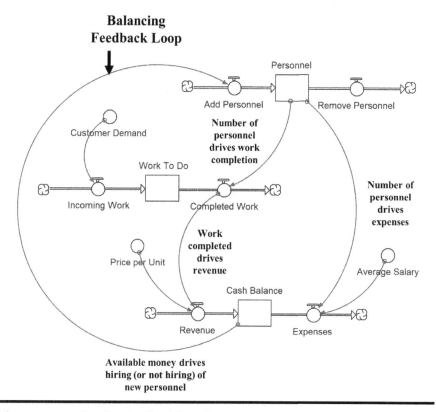

Figure 7.14   Balancing feedback loop in company system dynamics model.

(in this simple, limited example). The amounts of *Revenue* and *Expenses* impact the *Cash Balance*, which then determines how much money is available to *Add Personnel*. If a lot of money is available, more employees will be added to keep up with the high customer demand. If not much money is available, fewer employees will be added. If the company is losing money, employees may even be removed to decrease costs to match the lower level of customer demand. This balancing feedback loop aims to keep the number of employees at a level that is commensurate with the amount of available funds in the company (which is partially driven by customer demand).

Some Final Comments on System Dynamics Modeling

The SD modeling and simulation approach is growing in its popularity for addressing organization, managerial, and social issues. First, the models are more realistic, because they capture cause-and-effect linkages, feedback loops, delays, non-linear relationships, and decision-making policies. Second, the simulations are more accurate and reliable, because they provide a sanity check on assumptions, are more rigorous than mental models or spreadsheets, allow analysis of a wider range of issues, and identify the actions that are most effective (and least effective). Third, SD models can incorporate "soft" variables as stocks, much like the "hard" variable *Cash Balance* in Figure 7.12. For instance, an SD model for a company may capture the "level of customer satisfaction" based on activities, which may, in turn, affect the "probability of buying again." Both "level of customer satisfaction" and "probability of buying again" are variables that can accumulate. Customer satisfaction can be high or low, and a probability can be high or low. Thus, they can each be represented by a stock in an SD model, and the flows into and out of those stocks can be based on elements that might change the "amount" in each stock.

With numerous interconnected activities, management of organizational or social systems is extremely difficult and complex. Understanding the dynamic behavior of any large, complex system like this is typically beyond human comprehension. Instead, each entity or business group in the overall system understands its small part of the system in great detail, but no single entity has an overarching view of the entire system. Without an understanding of the entire system, its components, and their interactions, it is impossible to know what the best long-term global decisions are. This causes local sub-optimization, as each entity seeks to improve its part of the system without full knowledge of its interconnections with, and influences on, other entities in the system. Even with the best intentions, this type of situation can be burdened by low performance and frustration.

Like natural ecosystems, organizations themselves are ecosystems, with many checks and balances occurring. These checks and balances typically manifest themselves as management policies or actions. For example, when organizational spending exceeds the proposed budget, management actions are typically taken to bring costs back down to the budgeted amount. Or, if a new product is not selling well, management actions are typically taken to remove that product from the portfolio offered by the organization. These management actions are feedback loops, just like those that occur in natural ecosystems, and complex organizational systems are full of them. This makes management very difficult, because these feedback loops are interconnected, are non-linear, differ in strength, and operate over different time spans. A good example of feedback loops differing in strength and operating over different time spans is the traditional S-curve. The S-curve has been used to explain many phenomena, from a population of rabbits in a field to the adoption of a new technology. In an S-curve for the adoption of a new technology, the beginning upward momentum is the result of a positive, reinforcing feedback loop (e.g., word-of-mouth marketing). Then, after a period of time, the upward slope begins to flatten out as a result of a negative, balancing feedback loop (e.g., saturated market). Like a natural ecosystem, every organizational system seeks balance.

SD is a powerful structural modeling technique that can capture the feedback loops that drive the behavior of organizations or social systems over time, both in the short term and in the long term. Chapters 8 and 9 will walk through two examples of consequence maps that are translated into SD models when quantification is desired beyond the insights offered by a consequence map.

Bibliography

Forrester, Jay W., *Industrial Dynamics*, Cambridge, MA: Productivity Press, 1961.

Forrester, Jay W., *Collected Papers of Jay W. Forrester*, Cambridge, MA: Wright-Allen Press, 1975.

Pryor, Mildred G., White, J. Chris, and Toombs, Leslie, *Strategic Quality Management: A Strategic Systems Approach to Continuous Improvement*, Boston, MA: Cengage Learning, 2007.

Senge, Peter M., *The Fifth Discipline: The Art & Practice of the Learning Organization*, New York: Doubleday/Currency, 1990.

Sterman, J. D., *Business Dynamics: Systems Thinking and Modeling for a Complex World*, New York: Irwin/McGraw-Hill, 2000.

White, J. Chris and Sholtes, Robert M., *The Dynamic Progress Method: Using Advanced Simulation to Improve Project Planning and Management*, Boca Raton, FL: CRC Press, 2016.

Chapter 8

Example Simulation for Reduction in Force (RIF)

This chapter walks through the consequence map for an organization and the subsequent simulation to quantify the impacts of a large reduction in force (RIF). The purpose of this effort was to understand the risks associated with reducing the workforce in an organization by a significant amount. The organization, the Branding and Collaboration Group (BAC) within a service agency, had approximately 100 employees (called *associates*), and the organization was considering letting 20 people go (20% of workforce), reducing the workforce down to about 80 associates.

In any workforce-related organizational system, there is one overbearing feedback loop that exists: the balance of supply and demand. Figure 8.1 portrays this with a simple loop that shows that the *Demand for work* affects the *Capacity to do work*, and the *Capacity to do work* then affects the *Demand for work*. In the end, the organizational system is trying to balance these two elements.

However, the simple feedback loop in Figure 8.1 is not enough to guide the organization in any detail. It is a useful concept but not practical. Therefore, the simple feedback loop needs to be expanded into a larger consequence map.

The Full Consequence Map

Similarly to Chapters 5 and 6 in Section II, in this chapter, we will start with the overall completed consequence map and then describe the key feedback loops that drive the system. Figure 8.2 shows the full consequence map that resulted from the analysis. Start with *Customer Demand* in the upper left of the diagram.

127

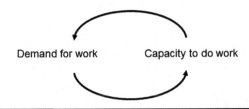

Figure 8.1   Overall balancing feedback loop of supply and demand.

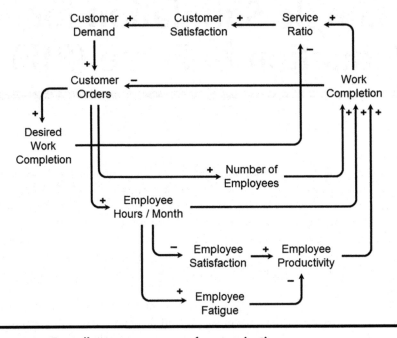

Figure 8.2   Overall consequence map for organization.

The customers for the BAC group are both internal and external to the company. *Customer Demand* manifests itself through *Customer Orders*. These elements move in the same direction, indicated by the + sign on the arrow: the more demand there is, the more orders there are (or, the less demand there is, the fewer orders there are). The *Customer Orders* lead to a *Desired Work Completion* (+ on the arrow). For example, if there were 100 orders, the group would desire to complete 100 orders. If there were 10 orders, the group would desire to complete the 10 orders. The *Desired Work Completion* sets up an expectation, which will be discussed in more detail when the *Service Ratio* is discussed.

Another arrow comes out of *Customer Orders* and goes to *Employee Hours/Month*. These elements move in the same direction (+ sign on arrow). The more *Customer Orders* there are, the more *Employee Hours/Month* are needed to accomplish the work. Remember, for consequence maps, each arrow of causality is treated individually, so that *Employee Hours/Month* would increase, assuming all other elements stayed the same. As can be seen, yet another arrow comes out of *Customer Orders* and goes into *Number of Employees* (same direction, + on arrowhead). As *Customer Orders* increase, the *Number of Employees* must also increase (over time) to accomplish more work. Consequently, there are two ways to increase the amount of work accomplished by the group: increase the *Number of Employees* or increase the *Employee Hours/Month*, or a combination of both. For instance, if a typical customer order requires 4 hours of work, each person could do two orders per day (8 hours/day ÷ 4 hours/order = 2 orders/day). If the group has 10 people in it, then 20 orders per day could be completed (10 employees × 2 orders/day/employee = 20 orders/day). If the number of orders per day increases from 20 to 30, then there are multiple ways to increase the work to accomplish the 30 orders per day. Here are three examples:

1. Increase the *Employee Hours/Month* so that all group employees work 12 hours/day instead of 8 hours/day:
   (12 hours/day/employee × 10 employees) ÷ 4 hours/order = 30 orders/day

2. Increase the *Number of Employees* from 10 to 15 while maintaining an 8 hour work day:
   (8 hours/day/employee × 15 employees) ÷ 4 hours/order = 30 orders/day

3. Increase the *Employee Hours/Month* so that all group employees work 10 hours/day, and increase the *Number of Employees* from 10 to 12:
   (10 hours/day × 12 employees) ÷ 4 hours/order = 30 orders/day

As shown in these three examples, the product of *Employee Hours/Month* and *Number of Employees* leads to *Work Completion*. The first thing that happens with *Work Completion* is that the backlog of *Customer Orders* is decreased (a − sign on the arrowhead), because work is accomplished. Next, the amount of work completed by the group (i.e., *Work Completion*) is compared with the *Desired Work Completion* in the *Service Ratio* to determine how well the group did with regard to satisfying *Customer Demand*. If we represent the *Service Ratio* as the ratio of *Work Completion* to *Desired Work Completion* (i.e., *Work Completion/Desired Work Completion*), then a ratio of 1.0 indicates that the group exactly met the level of demand from the customer (i.e., *Work Completion* = *Desired Work Completion*). A ratio less than 1.0 indicates that the group *did not* meet the demand from the customer (i.e., *Work Completion* < *Desired Work Completion*). Because the smaller number (*Work Completion*) is in the numerator and the larger number (*Desired Work Completion*) is in the denominator, we have a fraction less than 1. On the other hand, a ratio greater than 1.0 indicates that the group *exceeded* the demand from the customer (i.e., *Work Completion* > *Desired Work Completion*). Because the larger number (*Work Completion*) is in the numerator and the smaller number

(*Desired Work Completion*) is in the denominator, we have a fraction greater than 1. For this reason, the arrow from *Work Completion* to *Service Ratio* has a + on the end to indicate that an increase in *Work Completion* leads to an increase in *Service Ratio* (assuming the *Desired Work Completion* remains the same). And, the arrow from *Desired Work Completion* has a − on the end to indicate that an increase in *Desired Work Completion* leads to a decrease in *Service Ratio* (assuming the *Work Completion* remains the same).

The *Service Ratio* (over time) has a direct impact on *Customer Satisfaction*. If the group continues to meet or exceed the demand from customers, then customers will tend to be satisfied. In other words, if the *Service Ratio* is greater than 1.0, then *Customer Satisfaction* will tend to be high. (Notice that this does not include any element related to the "quality" of the work accomplished. The consequence map could easily be expanded to include such elements.) Conversely, if the *Service Ratio* (over time) is low (i.e., less than 1.0), then the *Customer Satisfaction* will tend to be low. Finally, *Customer Satisfaction* drives *Customer Demand*. Higher *Customer Satisfaction* leads to higher *Customer Demand*, and eventually, lower *Customer Satisfaction* leads to lower *Customer Demand*.

Going back to *Employee Hours/Month*, there are two additional arrows coming out of *Employee Hours/Month* going into *Employee Satisfaction* and *Employee Fatigue*. As the work time for employees increases, over a period of time, *Employee Satisfaction* will tend to decrease (a − sign on the arrow), because people do not like to work excessively beyond the typical 8 hour day. A decrease in *Employee Satisfaction* then leads to a decrease in *Employee Productivity* (a + sign on the arrow), which leads to a decrease in *Work Completion*. Using the work capacity calculations earlier in this section, consider the initial example of 10 employees working 8 hours/day to complete 20 orders/day. A fundamental assumption in this calculation is that the employees are at their "normal" level of productivity, such that *Employee Productivity* = 1 (or 100%). The calculation should really be

$$(10 \text{ employees} \times 8 \text{ hours/day/employee} \times 1.0) / 4 \text{ hours/order} = 20 \text{ orders/day}$$

If *Employee Productivity* drops, such as *Employee Productivity* = 0.75 (or 75%), a lower number of orders would be completed:

$$(10 \text{ employees} \times 8 \text{ hours/day/employee} \times 0.75) \div 4 \text{ hours/order} = 15 \text{ orders/day}$$

Now, work capacity is a function of the *Number of Employees*, the amount of time the employees work (*Employee Hours/Month*), and the average *Employee Productivity*.

In addition, as the work time for employees increases (*Employee Hours/Month*), eventually, the level of *Employee Fatigue* will increase (a + sign on the arrow). The more employees work over a period of time, the more burned out (fatigued) they will become. People are not robots. Take the extreme example of working 24 hours/day.

A person will become extremely fatigued in this situation and will require some kind of rest. A person cannot sustain this level of work forever. At a lower level, this still happens when people work 10 to 12 hours a day. The fatigue is not as high as the extreme example of working 24 hours/day (in which case fatigue would go to 100%, and the person would be completely physically and mentally fatigued and would have to stop), but there is still some level of fatigue. The level of *Employee Fatigue* has an inversely proportional relationship to *Employee Productivity* (a − sign on the arrow). The more fatigued a person becomes, the less productive that person becomes. Again, consider the 24 hour example. After 24 hours, a person might be completely fatigued (*Employee Fatigue* = 100%), and the person is completely useless and cannot physically or mentally function, because he or she is sleeping (*Employee Productivity* = 0%). Of course, someone might actually make it to 1 or 2 days under these conditions, based on their constitution and endurance, but the point here is that eventually, someone can be driven to such a level of fatigue that the human body just ceases to function, because it has to rest.

The Feedback Loops

In this consequence map, there are four key feedback loops:

- Balancing feedback loop for business size (Figure 8.3)
- Reinforcing feedback loop for business growth (Figure 8.4)
- Balancing feedback loop for the workload of the employees (Figure 8.5)
- Reinforcing feedback loop for employee productivity (Figure 8.6)

Figure 8.3 highlights the balancing (negative) feedback loop (odd number of − signs) that controls the amount of *Customer Demand* based on the ability of the group to accomplish work (*Service Ratio*). Essentially, the level of *Customer Demand* will eventually settle at the level at which the group can adequately accomplish work (*Service Ratio* = 1.0). If the group can only complete 20 orders/day, then eventually *Customer Demand* will be roughly 20 orders/day. If the group can complete more, then the *Service Ratio* will be higher (> 1.0) for a while, which will tend to increase *Customer Satisfaction* and *Customer Demand* to the point where the *Service Ratio* reaches 1.0 again. If *Customer Demand* is high and the *Service Ratio* is low (< 1.0), then *Customer Satisfaction* will decrease along with *Customer Demand* down to such a level that the *Service Ratio* can recover to 1.

Figure 8.4 shows the "business growth" reinforcing (positive) feedback loop (zero − signs). In this feedback loop, the *Customer Demand* increases (or decreases) based on increases in the size of the work capacity of the group (represented by the combination of *Number of Employees* and *Employee Hours/Month*). When *Customer Demand* increases, and the group responds with an increase in work capacity (which will get the *Service Ratio* up to 1.0 or higher), then *Customer Demand* will

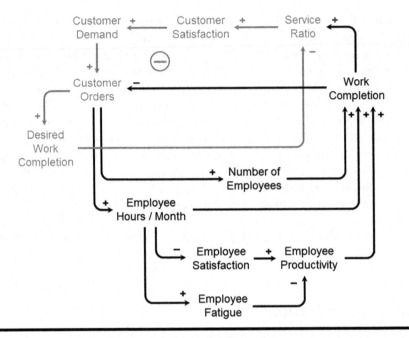

Figure 8.3   Balancing feedback loop for business size.

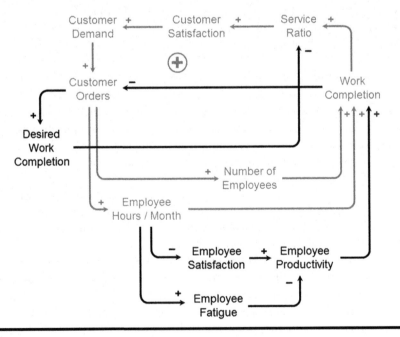

Figure 8.4   Reinforcing feedback loop for business growth.

continue to grow. In the opposite direction, if the work capacity shrinks, then eventually, the *Customer Demand* will also shrink (because the *Service Ratio* will be less than 1).

Figure 8.5 gives the balancing (negative) feedback loop (odd number of – signs) for the size of the workload for the employees based on *Customer Demand* (through *Customer Orders*). As *Customer Orders* increase (or decrease), the group needs more (or less) work capacity (the product of the *Number of Employees* and the *Employees Hours/Month*) to drive how much work gets completed (*Work Completion*) compared with the demand level (*Customer Orders*). If not enough work is getting completed, then the work capacity is increased. If too much work is getting completed, then the work capacity is decreased.

Figure 8.6 highlights the reinforcing (positive) feedback loop (even number of – signs) caused by *Employee Productivity*. The level of productivity for the employees in the group is based on their workload, which is based on the *Customer Orders*. This represents the vicious loop that can happen in organizations. More orders lead to more work, which leads to less productivity and less work accomplished. (Notice that this could also be represented as a balancing [negative] feedback loop if a comparison were made with a normal 8 hour day. In such a balancing feedback loop, the level of *Customer Orders* would decrease [or increase] based on whether or not people were working more [or less] than 8 hours/day.)

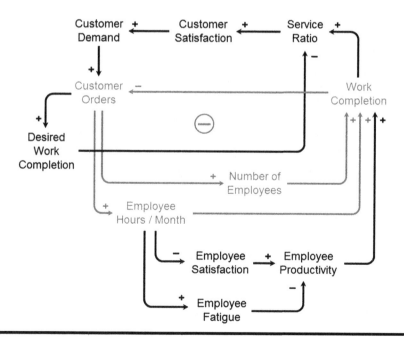

Figure 8.5   Balancing feedback loop for employee workload.

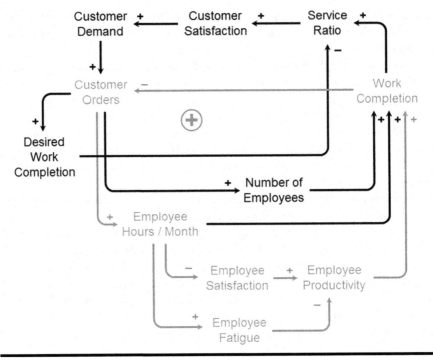

Figure 8.6   Reinforcing feedback loop for productivity impacts.

The Simulation Model

Chapter 7 provided an overview of the system dynamics (SD) simulation approach. As stated in Chapter 7, this book is not intended to provide full instructions for developing SD simulations. In this chapter, the reader will see how the consequence map in Figure 8.2 migrated into an SD simulation model, and how this model was used to test several what-if scenarios. In this simulation, the true numbers have been replaced with fictitious numbers to protect the sensitivity of the project. Yet, this replacement has been done in such a way that the dynamics provide the same dynamics and conclusions as in the real-world project.

Figure 8.7 shows the portion of the SD model related to various customer variables. In the model, the single stock called *Service Orders Backlog* represents the *Customer Orders* part of the consequence map in Figure 8.2. The model begins in the upper left of the diagram with an exogenous variable called *Normal Customer Demand* (which is a steady demand stream of 12 orders/month) that provides the input to *Customer Demand*, which then provides input to a flow called *Incoming Orders*. The inflow *Incoming Orders* flows into the stock called *Service Orders Backlog*, which represents unfulfilled customer orders. The outflow called *Completed Orders* represents the orders that have been fulfilled, which depletes the *Service Orders*

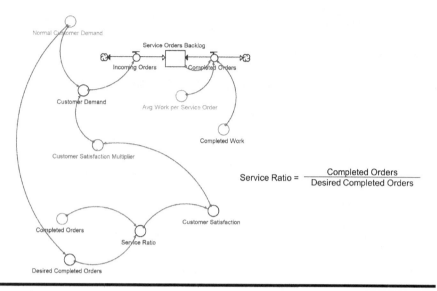

Figure 8.7 Simulation model for customer interfaces.

Backlog. The outflow *Completed Orders* is driven by *Completed Work* (which is in another part of the model). (Note: Variables with dashed-line circles are "ghosted" from another part of the model. The ghosting technique is used to maintain clarity of the model diagram, to avoid numerous lines crossing other lines or variables.) These variables (*Incoming Orders*, *Service Orders Backlog*, and *Completed Orders*) provide the main flow for this portion of the model, and so far, it represents the connection between *Customer Demand* and *Customer Orders* from Figure 8.2, as well as the decrease in *Customer Orders* due to *Work Completion*.

The variable *Normal Customer Demand* also provides input to the variable *Desired Completed Orders* (which, of course, relates to *Desired Work Completion* in Figure 8.2). *Desired Completed Orders* and *Completed Orders* both go to *Service Ratio* (just as *Desired Work Completion* and *Work Completion* go into *Service Ratio* in the consequence map). The formula on the right side of the diagram in Figure 8.7 matches the formula provided in the previous section for *Service Ratio*:

Service Ratio = Completed Orders/Desired Completed Orders (in the SD model)

$$\text{Service Ratio} = \text{Work Completion}/\text{Desired Work Completion}$$
$$(\text{in the consequence map})$$

The *Service Ratio* then provides input into the variable *Customer Satisfaction*, as in Figure 8.2. *Customer Satisfaction* provides input to a variable called *Customer Satisfaction Multiplier*, which then impacts *Customer Demand*. Thus,

Customer Demand is a combination of a steady-state *Normal Customer Demand* with a multiplier on it to shift it up and down based on the level of *Customer Satisfaction*.

$$\text{Customer Demand} = \text{Normal Customer Demand}$$
$$\times \text{Customer Satisfaction Multiplier}$$

The use of multipliers is a common method in SD to provide feedback from one variable to another. Based on the value of one variable, the multiplying effect on another variable may be larger, small, or nothing (multiplier = 1.0). Furthermore, this relationship is typically non-linear, so that a change of 2× for the input does not necessarily result in a 2× multiplier (but perhaps a 2.7× multiplier).

Finally, the *Customer Demand* (perhaps changed based on the *Customer Satisfaction Multiplier*) then provides another input into *Incoming Orders* in the next time step of the simulation, and the feedback loop is complete from *Customer Demand* to *Service Orders Backlog* to *Service Ratio* back to *Customer Demand*, as in Figure 8.3.

Figure 8.8 shows the part of the SD model that relates to *Work Completion*. This part of the model has three stocks: *Work Backlog* (similar to *Service Orders Backlog*), *BAC Labor*, and *Hours per Month per Person*. This part of the model starts with the ghosted variable *Incoming Orders* from the customer model in Figure 8.7. *Incoming Orders* leads to the inflow *Incoming Work*. In this model, each order is 100 hours of work (*Avg Work per Service Order*), so the orders are multiplied by 100 to get a total number of hours of work incoming to the group. In the steady state, demand is 12 orders/month, which equates to 1200 hours of work (12 orders/month * 100 hours/orders = 1200 hours/month).

Incoming Work goes into the stock *Work Backlog*, and *Completed Work* is the outflow from this stock, which represents a decrease in the *Work Backlog* as work is accomplished. Notice that *Completed Work* (through the variable *Effective BAC Labor*) is based on *BAC Labor*, *Hours per Month per Person*, and *Effective BAC Labor Productivity*, similarly to the consequence map in which *Work Completion* is based on *Number of Employees*, *Employee Hours/Month*, and *Employee Productivity*. *Incoming Work* is also an input for the variable *Required Hrs per Mo per Person* (required hours per month per person). The *Required Hrs per Mo per Person* controls the inflows to the stocks *Hours per Month per Person* and *BAC Labor*. In the consequence map in Figure 8.2, this is the connection between *Customer Orders* and *Employee Hours/Month* and *Number of Employees*, respectively. This connection in the model represents how the number of hours and employees are changed based on the incoming customer demand.

For the stock *BAC Labor*, the inflow is *BAC Labor In* (adding employees), and the outflow is *BAC Labor Out* (removing employees). For each of these flows, there is a delay for the activity to happen (*BAC Labor In Delay* and *BAC Labor Out Delay*) to show that employees cannot be hired and trained immediately, and

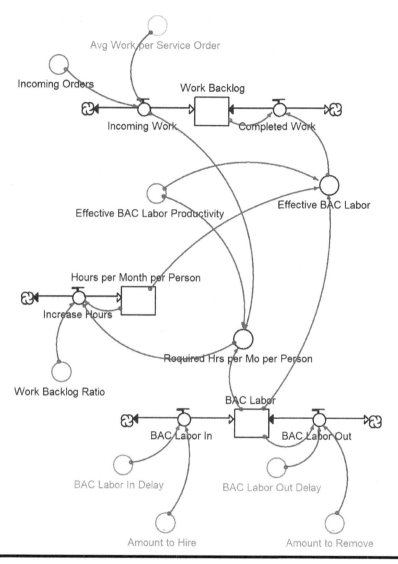

Figure 8.8   Simulation model for service delivery.

sometimes, there is a delay in removing employees (e.g., filling out proper paper-work, checking for other options, reviewing legal implications, etc.). For each of these flows, there is also an amount to add or remove (*Amount to Hire* and *Amount to Remove*). In the simulation, the amount that is to be added or removed is spread over the delay time period. For example, if 30 people were going to be added with a delay of 3 months (for recruiting and selection), then 10 people for the next three simulation time periods would go through the inflow (*BAC Labor In*) into the stock *BAC Labor*.

The stock *Hours per Month per Person* (same as *Employee Hours/Month* in the consequence map) is altered by the combined inflow/outflow variable called *Increase Hours*. This variable is positive when hours are added and negative when hours are removed. (This is the same calculation as having a separate inflow and outflow, as with the other stocks.) The variable *Increase Hours* is also driven by the *Work Backlog Ratio*, which is a ghosted variable from another part of the model (the part of the model shown in Figure 8.9).

The part of the model shown in Figure 8.8 covers the two feedback loops in Figures 8.4 and 8.5. In both of these feedback loops, the work capacity of the group, related to the *Number of Employees* and *Employee Hours/Month* in the consequence map (*BAC Labor* and *Hours per Month per Person* in the simulation model), is driven by the *Customer Orders* in the consequence map (*Incoming Orders* in the simulation model), which covers the feedback loop in Figure 8.5. *Completed Work* then gets passed on (ghosted) to the part of the model in Figure 8.7 to complete the feedback loop shown in Figure 8.4.

Figure 8.9 shows the final part of the SD model related to satisfaction and productivity. (Note: *Fatigue* was not included in this particular model.) *Associate Satisfaction* (same as *Employee Satisfaction* in the consequence map) is

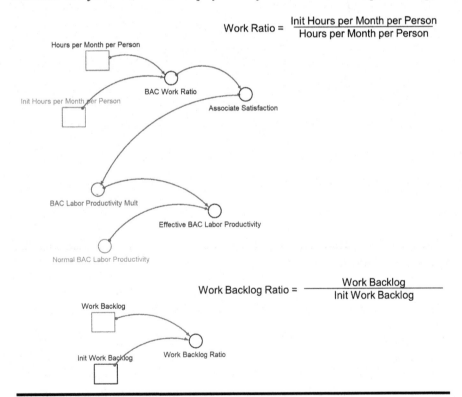

$$\text{Work Ratio} = \frac{\text{Init Hours per Month per Person}}{\text{Hours per Month per Person}}$$

$$\text{Work Backlog Ratio} = \frac{\text{Work Backlog}}{\text{Init Work Backlog}}$$

Figure 8.9   Simulation model for employee factors.

based on the *BAC Work Ratio*, which is the ratio of the initial hours per month that people are working (*Init Hours per Month per Person*) to the current hours per month that people are working (*Hours per Month per Person*). The model starts off with everyone working a "normal" month of 160 hours (approximately 40 hours per week for 4 weeks). As the ratio gets smaller, because the employees are working more hours per month than at the beginning of the simulation (normal hours), there is an impact on *Associate Satisfaction*. The *Associate Satisfaction* then has an impact on *Effective BAC Labor Productivity* through the multiplier called *BAC Labor Productivity Mult*. This multiplier value is multiplied by the *Normal BAC Labor Productivity* (assumed to be 75%) to give a new value for productivity.

In Figure 8.8, notice that the *Work Backlog Ratio* does not impact the number of employees as it does in the consequence map. For this analysis, the focus was on specifically controlling the inflow and outflow of labor to test the impact of a change in the size of the workforce on the rest of the model (since the focus was on a reduction in force).

Figures 8.10 and 8.11 provide the output of the simulation for the baseline run. In the baseline model, the following initial values are used:

Simulation time step = 1 month
Length of simulation = 24 months (2 years)
Normal Customer Demand = 12 orders per month
Avg Work per Service Order = 100 hours per order
BAC Labor In Delay = 3 months
BAC Labor Out Delay = 2 months
Amount to Hire = 0 persons per month (i.e., no hiring)
Amount to Remove = 0 persons per month (i.e., no removal of people)
Init Hours per Month per Person = 160 hours/month/person
Normal BAC Labor Productivity = 0.75 (75%)
BAC Labor = 10 associates

Based on these initial values, the initial amount of work coming into the group is

Incoming Work = Normal Customer Demand × Avg Work per Service Order

Incoming Work = 12 orders/month × 100 hours/order = 1200 hours/month

The initial amount of work completed by the group is

Completed Work = BAC Labor × Init Hours per Month per Person
× Normal BAC Labor Productivity

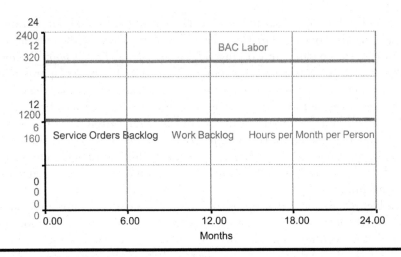

Figure 8.10   Simulation results for baseline (part 1).

Figure 8.11   Simulation results for baseline (part 2).

$$\text{Completed Work} = 10 \text{ people} \times 160 \text{ hours/month/person} \times 0.75$$
$$= 12 \text{ hours/month}$$

Notice that for the baseline run, the *Incoming Work* equals the *Completed Work* (at 1200 hours/month). This ensures that the stock called *Work Backlog* remains constant. If the stock *Work Backlog* remains constant, and the stock *BAC Labor* remains constant (as described above with zero values for *Amount to Hire* and *Amount to Remove*), then the model will stay in equilibrium. Nothing will change, because there are no perturbations to kick off the feedback loops. In SD simulations, initializing the model in equilibrium is extremely important, so that any changes in model behavior will be completely due to the changes purposely made later in the simulation (e.g., removing employees to represent a reduction in force).

In Figure 8.10, there are four lines for the four stocks: *BAC Labor*, *Service Orders Backlog*, *Work Backlog*, and *Hours per Month per Person*. The scales on the vertical axis are

Scale for *BAC Labor*: 0 to 12 (current value at 10)
Scale for *Service Orders Backlog*: 0 to 24 (current value at 12, the mid-line)
Scale for *Work Backlog*: 0 to 2400 (current value at 1200, the mid-line)
Scale for *Hours per Month per Person*: 0 to 320 (current value at 160, the mid-line)

Figure 8.10 shows that all stocks in the model stay constant at the values in the list directly above.

In Figure 8.11, there are three lines for three other key variables that drive feedback loops: *Customer Satisfaction*, *Associate Satisfaction*, and *Work Backlog Ratio*. The scales on the vertical axis are

Scale for *Customer Satisfaction*: 0 to 200 (current value at 100, the mid-line)
Scale for *Associate Satisfaction*: 0 to 200 (current value at 100, the mid-line)
Scale for *Work Backlog Ratio*: 0 to 2 (current value at 1, the mid-line)

Figure 8.11 shows that all stocks in the model stay constant at the values in the list directly above. For *Customer Satisfaction* and *Associate Satisfaction*, the scale on the graph is 0 to 200, but the value will never go above 100 (such as 100%). Thus, the baseline simulation shows that customers are very happy (100% satisfaction), and associates are very happy (100% satisfaction). The *Work Backlog Ratio* begins and stays at 1.0, because everything is in steady state, and the *Work Backlog* at any point in the simulation is still equal to the *Init Work Backlog*.

Simulation Scenarios and Results

For the following scenarios, the simulation runs will begin with the same equilibrium values as shown in the baseline simulation (considered to be Scenario 1). However, some changes will be introduced at a later time step in the simulation, and the change in the output will be a direct result of the change.

In the second what-if scenario, the workforce is purposely reduced by 20% (from 10 associates to 8 associates) in Month 5 of the simulation to represent a reduction in force. However, the effects of any changes in *Customer Satisfaction* and *Associate Satisfaction* are "turned off" to isolate the changes in other variables. That is, the feedback loops based on changes in these two variables are constrained, so that they have no effect on other variables. Figure 8.12 shows this immediate drop in *BAC Labor*. As a result, the *Work Backlog* increases for a while, as the *Hours per Month per Person* ramp up to meet the new demand on the remaining associates. Eventually, the *Hours per Month per Person* levels out at a new equilibrium of 200 hours/month/person.

Hours per Month per Person = Work Backlog/

(BAC Labor × Effective BAC Labor Productivity)

Hours per Month per Person = 1200 hours/month/(8 people × 0.75)

= 200 hours/month/person

The *Service Orders Backlog* line follows the *Work Backlog* line.

Figure 8.13 shows the results for the other three key variables. The *Work Backlog Ratio* follows similar behavior to the *Work Backlog* and *Service Orders Backlog* in Figure 8.12. It rises for a while and then settles back down to 1 as associates work more hours to get all the work completed. As the *Work Backlog Ratio* rises (which indicates that the group is not getting as much work done as at the beginning of the simulation), there is a dip in *Customer Satisfaction*, which begins to recover as the *Work Backlog Ratio* stops increasing. The reduction in force in Month 5 also causes a dip in *Associate Satisfaction* as associates increase their *Hours per Month per Person*. As stated at the beginning of this scenario, there are no impacts due to the drops in *Customer Satisfaction* and *Associate Satisfaction*.

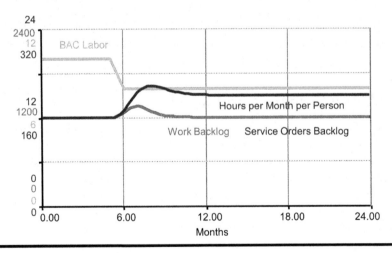

Figure 8.12 Simulation results for Scenario 2 (part 1).

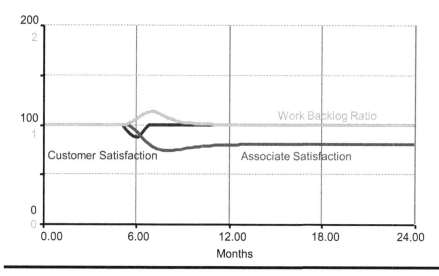

Figure 8.13   Simulation results for Scenario 2 (part 2).

Figure 8.14 compares the results for *Associate Satisfaction* for the baseline simulation run (Scenario 1) and this Scenario 2. As one would expect, the *Associate Satisfaction* drops and stays lower than the baseline value, because associates are unhappy that they are working 25% more hours (160 hours/month/person increased to 200 hours/month/person). Because the first scenario is set up so that the feedback loop for *Associate Satisfaction* is disabled, there are no negative effects of the reduction in force. Unfortunately, this is how many corporate managers often view

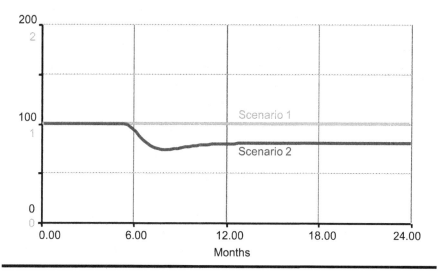

Figure 8.14   Comparison of associate satisfaction.

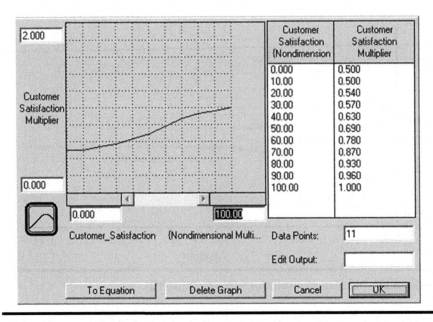

Figure 8.15   Multiplier table function for customer demand.

reductions in force. There are no significant impacts. The organization can lower costs with no impacts to work accomplished or the customers' perception.

The third what-if scenario is the same as Scenario 2, but the feedback loop for *Customer Satisfaction* is turned on, so that there is an impact on *Customer Demand* due to the decrease in *Customer Satisfaction*. (Note: The feedback loop for *Associate Satisfaction* is still turned off.) Figure 8.15 shows the table function that makes this happen. The table function provides the multiplier on *Customer Demand* based on the value of *Customer Satisfaction*. Looking at the table on the right of Figure 8.15, when *Customer Satisfaction* (left column) is 100 (i.e., 100%, perfectly happy), the multiplier on *Customer Demand* (right column) is 1 (i.e., no change in demand). When *Customer Satisfaction* is 70 (i.e., 70%), the multiplier on *Customer Demand* is 0.87 (i.e., demand is 87% of the initial demand). And when *Customer Satisfaction* is 50 (i.e., 50%), the multiplier on *Customer Demand* is 0.69 (i.e., demand is 69% of the initial demand). The line on the graph on the left of Figure 8.15 shows this relationship graphically. Notice that it is not a straight line. The relationship between *Customer Satisfaction* and *Customer Demand* is not linear.

Figures 8.16 and 8.17 show the results for Scenario 3. In Figure 8.16, the changes in the four stocks are shown. For comparison purposes, a dotted line is shown for the *Hours per Month per Person* for Scenario 2. Now, the temporary decrease in *Customer Satisfaction* reduces *Customer Demand*, which slightly decreases the workload on associates during the ramp-up. The decreased *Work Backlog* means that not as many *Hours per Month per Person* are required as in Scenario 2, but the decrease is insignificant.

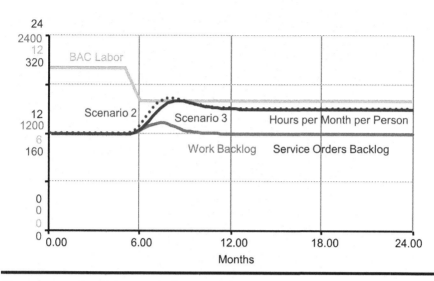

Figure 8.16   Simulation results for Scenario 3 (part 1).

In Figure 8.17, the dotted line for Scenario 2 is for *Associate Satisfaction*. A lower value for *Hours per Month per Person* results in a slightly higher *Associate Satisfaction* level in Scenario 3 as compared with Scenario 2. There is also a slight decrease in the *Work Backlog Ratio* (and *Work Backlog*) and a slight increase in *Customer Satisfaction*, but they are too small to see on the graph, so they are not highlighted.

In the fourth scenario, the impacts of *Associate Satisfaction* are isolated. Thus, the feedback loop for *Associate Satisfaction* is turned on, and the feedback loop for

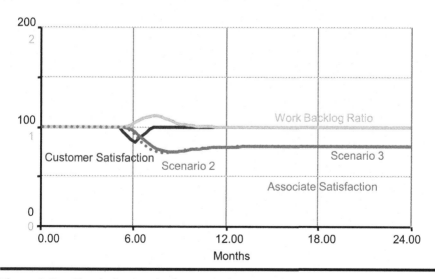

Figure 8.17   Simulation results for Scenario 3 (part 2).

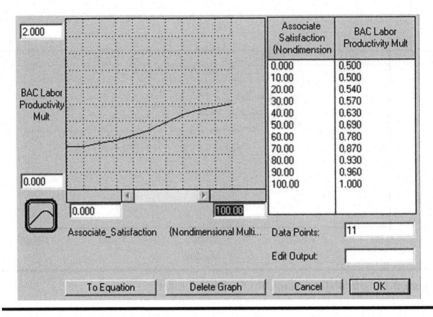

The table on the right shows:

Associate Satisfaction (Nondimension	BAC Labor Productivity Mult
0.000	0.500
10.00	0.500
20.00	0.540
30.00	0.570
40.00	0.630
50.00	0.690
60.00	0.780
70.00	0.870
80.00	0.930
90.00	0.960
100.00	1.000

Figure 8.18 **Multiplier table function for BAC labor productivity.**

Customer Satisfaction is turned off again. Scenario 4 is the same as Scenario 2, but now just the *Associate Satisfaction* feedback loop is turned on. Figure 8.18 shows the table function that makes this happen. The table function provides the multiplier on *BAC Labor Productivity* based on the value of *Associate Satisfaction*. Looking at the table on the right of Figure 8.18, when *Associate Satisfaction* (left column) is 100 (i.e., 100%, perfectly happy), the multiplier on *BAC Labor Productivity* (right column) is 1 (i.e., no change in productivity). Similarly to the table in Figure 8.15, when *Associate Satisfaction* is 70 (i.e., 70%), the multiplier on *BAC Labor Productivity* is 0.87 (i.e., productivity is 87% of the initial productivity). And when *Associate Satisfaction* is 50 (i.e., 50%), the multiplier on *BAC Labor Productivity* is 0.69 (i.e., productivity is 69% of the initial productivity). The line on the graph on the left of Figure 8.15 shows this relationship graphically. As in Figure 8.15, notice that it is not a straight line. The relationship between *Associate Satisfaction* and *BAC Labor Productivity* is not linear.

Figures 8.19 and 8.20 show the results for Scenario 4. Similarly to Figure 8.16, for comparison purposes, a dotted line is shown for the *Hours per Month per Person* for Scenario 2. Notice the much larger increase in *Hours per Month per Person* for Scenario 4. The decrease in *BAC Labor Productivity* due to the lower *Associate Satisfaction* means that less work gets done, which requires even more *Hours per Month per Person* for the remaining associates. There is also a slight increase in *Work Backlog*, but it is too small to see on the graph.

Similarly to Figure 8.17, in Figure 8.19, the dotted line for Scenario 2 is for *Associate Satisfaction*. The larger increase in *Hours per Month per Person* for the

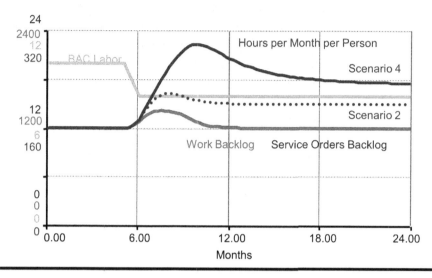

Figure 8.19 Simulation results for Scenario 4 (part 1).

remaining associates causes a further decrease in *Associate Satisfaction*, which causes a further decrease in *BAC Labor Productivity*. There is also a slight increase in *Work Backlog Ratio* (similar to *Work Backlog*) and a slight decrease in *Customer Satisfaction*, but these are too small to see on the graph.

As the reader can probably guess, the fifth scenario turns on *both* feedback loops for *Customer Satisfaction* and *Associate Satisfaction*. Thus, Scenario 5 is the same as Scenario 2 but with both feedback loops enabled. In Figure 8.21, the *Hours per Month per Person* is still high in Scenario 5 (compared with Scenario 2, the dotted

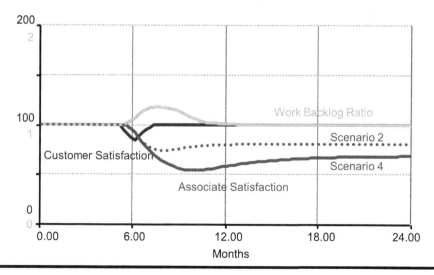

Figure 8.20 Simulation results for Scenario 4 (part 2).

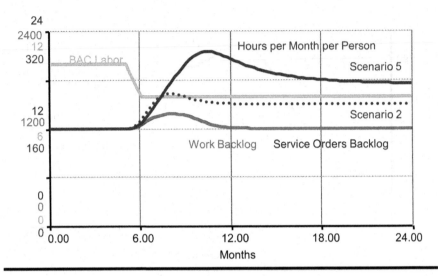

Figure 8.21 Simulation results for Scenario 5 (part 1).

line) but not as high as in Scenario 4, because the decrease in *Customer Satisfaction* reduces the *Customer Demand*, resulting in less work than in Scenario 4 for the remaining associates. In Figure 8.22, the increase in *Hours per Month per Person* for the remaining associates causes a decrease in *Associate Satisfaction*, which leads to lower *BAC Labor Productivity* and less work completed.

The results shown in Scenario 5 are the final results of analysis for this effort. The organization needed more than the qualitative insights of the consequence map in Figure 8.2. Instead, since the reduction in force was a very possible situation,

Figure 8.22 Simulation results for Scenario 5 (part 2).

the organization needed to know more precisely what might happen and when it might happen. How would delays in the system affect results? How would the interconnected feedback loops drive variables further than expected? Through this effort, the management of the organization learned that there is a very high risk associated with reducing workforce size due to budgetary constraints instead of changes in customer demand. Specifically, the same workload exists, but there will be fewer employees to handle that workload. This is fairly obvious to most people. But, the consequences of this higher workload on the employees are not often seriously considered in the decision, even though most people "know" that the remaining employees may not be too happy.

Based on this simple simulation, several ideas were discussed. First, the reduction could be spread out over a longer time period to spread out the impact. This would not eliminate the impact, but it would minimize it. For example, instead of reducing the workforce by 20% in a single reduction, there could be four reductions of 5% spread over several months. Second, outside contractors could be used to reduce the workload on the remaining employees. Of course, using outside contracts costs money, but for many skillsets, there are many options for hiring outside contractors that are less expensive than the cost of fully burdened employees (with benefits, etc.). Third, the organization could reduce customer demand to decrease the workload on the remaining employees. This idea was counterintuitive to a typical approach. Why would a business want to decrease its customer demand? Yet in terms of the "system," this is a viable solution. The price of the service provided by the organization could be increased, which would decrease demand a little while possibly keeping the same cash flow. For example, if the organization charges $100 for its service and there are 100 customers, the organization makes $10,000 in revenue. However, if the price is raised to $125 and the demand drops to 80 customers, the organization makes the same $10,000 in revenue while decreasing the workload on the remaining employees.

The organization used a combination of the first and third ideas: the reduction in force was spread out over 9 months, and the price of the service was slowly increased during that same time period. In the end, for the fiscal year in which this event occurred, the organization saw a change in revenue of +3%. In the previous 2 years, the organization had seen an average growth of +7%, so the +3% was much lower. However, the organization was very pleased that it did not lose any money and the remaining employees were as happy as, if not happier than, prior to the reduction in force.

Final Remarks

The consequence map for this project could have been bigger and involved more elements, but the scope of this consequence map and simulation captured sufficient dynamics and behavior to address the issue that the organization was facing. Possible additions to the system structure that were discussed by the team include outside contract labor, capital equipment used by the employees to provide their service, budget constraints, and connections to other groups in the organization. Possible additional relationships that could have been captured include other impacts of employee dissatisfaction (e.g., turnover, effects on the organization's reputation for hiring in the future, quality of work produced) and other impacts of customer dissatisfaction (e.g., organization's reputation, rework or "warranty" work).

Hopefully, this chapter showed the reader the next step beyond consequence maps and the benefits of simulation to show specific results and to test various what-if scenarios. In many cases, as shown in Chapters 4 through 6, the consequence map is enough to guide decision making. However, in the situations when additional details are needed before a decision can be made, the use of SD simulation is extremely powerful and effective.

Chapter 9

Example Simulation for Project Management

This chapter discusses a consequence map for a single project "task" and the subsequent simulation to quantify the impact of a very common management correction action called *crashing*, in which resources are added to a late project to get it back on schedule. There are two options for adding resources: adding overtime hours to current resources or adding more people, or a combination of both. The net effect is that more work hours are applied to the task to accelerate its schedule. The objective for this simulation is to understand how this specific management corrective action truly impacts the progression of work for a task on a project. In some instances, this corrective action is successful in getting a task back on track (i.e., getting a late task back on schedule). However, in other instances, this corrective action is not successful and somehow seems to worsen the problem (i.e., a late task falls even further behind schedule). Thus, the simulation is used to show which conditions would allow crashing to be successful as well as which conditions would cause crashing to be unsuccessful.

The Full Consequence Map

The consequence map for this example was published in a previous book by the author, *The Dynamic Progress Method: Using Advanced Simulation to Improve Project Planning and Management* (co-authors J. Chris White and Robert M. Sholtes, CRC Press, 2016, ISBN 9781466504370). Figure 9.1 shows this consequence map. However, this consequence map is not ideally suited to the descriptions that have been provided in this book. Instead, Figure 9.2 highlights the key elements of the underlying

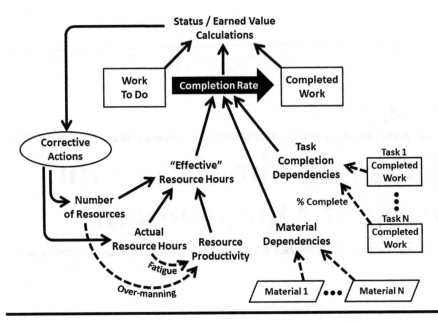

Figure 9.1 Overall consequence map for project task simulation. (From White, J. Chris and Sholtes, Robert M., *The Dynamic Progress Method: Using Advanced Simulation to Improve Project Planning and Management,* **CRC Press, 2016, figure 6.16, p. 132. With permission.)**

feedback loops and the signs on all the arrows. Notice in Figure 9.2 that a good deal of Figure 9.1 is removed. Figure 9.1 is for a larger, more sophisticated simulation of tasks for complex projects. For the purposes of this chapter, we will focus on just a few key feedback loops that operate at the "task" level (i.e., fully within the scope of a single task). These feedback loops consist of two primary crashing corrective actions taken by project managers when keeping a task on schedule and on budget.

In Figure 9.2, begin with *Work To Do. Work To Do* represents the backlog or stock of work that needs to be accomplished on this task, represented in labor hours (e.g., a 40-hour task). *Completion Rate* represents work accomplished, and it moves hours from *Work To Do* to *Completed Work.* For example, suppose that it is a 40-hour task. The initial *Work To Do* is 40 hours, and the initial *Completed Work* is 0 hours. After 1 day of work, suppose 8 hours of work were accomplished. This would move 8 hours from the bucket *Work To Do* to the bucket *Completed Work,* so that at the end of Day 1, *Work To Do* = 32 hours and *Completed Work* = 8 hours. Essentially, *Completion Rate* acts as a conveyor belt that moves hours from *Work To Do* to *Completed Work.* For this example, when the task is finished, *Work To Do* = 0 hours and *Completed Work* = 40 hours. As shown in Figure 9.2, the important element here is *Completion Rate.*

Three elements come together to provide the *"Effective" Resource Hours,* which drives the *Completion Rate: Number of Resources, Actual Resource Hours,* and

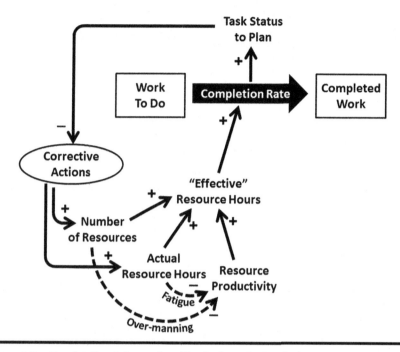

Figure 9.2   Key feedback loops for this single task simulation.

Resource Productivity. The *"Effective" Resource Hours* is the product of these three, exactly as was shown in Figure 8.2 for *Work Completion* for the reduction in force (RIF) example.

$$("Effective" Resource Hours = Number of Resources × Actual Resource Hours$$

$$× Resource Productivity)$$

As an example, if one person worked 8 hours in a day and was completely productive during those 8 hours (i.e., did not take any breaks, go to meetings, etc.), *"Effective" Resource Hours* would be the following:

"Effective" Resource Hours=1 person×8 hours/day/person×100%=8 hours/day

Each of these elements has the same type of impact on *"Effective" Resource Hours*, so there are + signs on all three arrows, because each element causes *"Effective" Resource Hours* to move in the same direction as the element.

The *Completion Rate* impacts the *Task Status to Plan*, which is the comparison of the status of the task (i.e., how much work has been completed by when) with the plan for the task. Continuing with the earlier example, if the plan showed completion of 8 hours on Day 1, then the task would be on schedule when compared with the plan. The *Task Status to Plan* is "better" (higher value) when the task completion is greater than what is stated in the plan, and *Task Status to Plan* is "worse" (lower value) when the task completion is smaller than what is stated in the plan. This is indicated by the + sign on the arrow. As the *Completion Rate* increases, the *Task Status to Plan* increases (assuming all other values stay the same). Or, as the *Completion Rate* decreases, the *Task Status to Plan* decreases.

Task Status to Plan then determines the *Corrective Actions*. In this case, *Corrective Actions* are taken to mean changes to the labor content (e.g., crashing). The "higher" the *Corrective Actions*, the more changes are made. Conversely, the "lower" the *Corrective Actions*, the fewer changes are made. Thus, there is a – sign on the arrow from *Task Status to Plan* to *Corrective Actions*, because these two elements move in opposite directions. When *Task Status to Plan* is high (i.e., ahead of the planned schedule), then *Corrective Actions* is low (i.e., no actions taken because the task is already doing well). However, when *Task Status to Plan* is low (i.e., late compared with the planned schedule), then *Corrective Actions* is high (i.e., lots of actions are taken, because the task needs to catch up).

Corrective Actions can then drive two changes, both in the same direction (+ signs on arrowheads). If *Corrective Actions* increases, there can be an increase in the *Number of Resources* (i.e., add some people to the task). Similarly, if *Corrective Actions* increases, there can also be an increase in the *Actual Resource Hours* (i.e., add overtime for the people working on the task). Or, the opposite can happen. When *Corrective Actions* is low, there are no changes to the *Number of Resources* or the *Actual Resource Hours*. Both *Number of Resources* and *Actual Resource Hours* can have opposite effects on the *Resource Productivity*. For the *Number of Resources*, this negative impact comes from *Over-manning* or putting too many people on the task. For some tasks, adding people just complicates things by adding more coordination effort (which takes away from productive task work), more training of the new people, more rework as the new people make mistakes, and so on. For the *Actual Resource Hours*, this negative impact comes from *Fatigue* or burnout. If someone works too many hours each day for an extended period of time, there will be physical consequences. Perhaps the person can handle working one day of overtime and come back the next day "fresh." Yet, if that same person works extensive overtime for several weeks in a row, the excess work takes a toll on the person, and they are not nearly as attentive, alert, and productive as when they are "fresh." This same negative connection between excessive employee work hours and employee productivity was also highlighted in the Chapter 8 example of the RIF.

The Feedback Loops

In this consequence map, there are four key feedback loops:

- Balancing feedback loop for *Number of Resources* (Figure 9.3)
- Balancing feedback loop for *Actual Resource Hours* (Figure 9.4)

- Reinforcing feedback loop for *Over-manning* (Figure 9.5)
- Reinforcing feedback loop for *Fatigue* (Figure 9.6)

Figure 9.3 shows the balancing (negative) feedback loop for *Number of Resources* highlighted in gray. It is a balancing (negative) feedback loop, because there is an odd number of – signs in the loop (only one, in this case). When the *Completion Rate* is low, the *Task Status to Plan* is low (i.e., the task is falling behind schedule), which kicks off more *Corrective Actions*. An increase in *Corrective Actions* leads to an increase in *Number of Resources*, which causes an increase in the *"Effective" Resource Hours*. The increase in *"Effective" Resource Hours* drives an increase in the *Completion Rate*, which also increases the *Task Status to Plan* (i.e., gets the task back on schedule). In this feedback loop, the *Number of Resources* is balanced to keep the task on schedule. As mentioned in the first paragraph of this chapter, this is a common management corrective action to take: add people to increase the amount of work accomplished to speed up the task progress.

Figure 9.4 shows the balancing (negative) feedback loop for *Actual Resource Hours*. It is very similar to the feedback loop in Figure 9.3 for *Number of Resources*. When the *Completion Rate* is low, the *Task Status to Plan* is low (i.e., the task is falling behind schedule), which kicks off more *Corrective Actions*. An increase in *Corrective Actions* leads to an increase in *Actual Resource Hours*, which causes an increase in the *"Effective" Resource Hours*. The increase in *"Effective" Resource Hours*

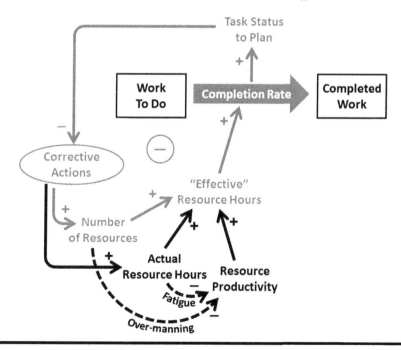

Figure 9.3 Balancing feedback loop for number of resources.

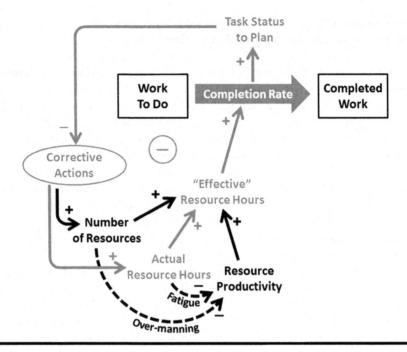

Figure 9.4 **Balancing feedback loop for actual resource hours.**

drives an increase in the *Completion Rate*, which also increases the *Task Status to Plan* (i.e., gets the task back on schedule). Just like the feedback loop in Figure 9.3, in this feedback loop, the *Actual Resource Hours* is balanced to keep the task on schedule. As mentioned in the first paragraph of this chapter, this is another very common management corrective action to take: make people work more to increase the amount of work accomplished to speed up the task progress.

Figure 9.5 shows the reinforcing (positive) feedback loop for *Over-manning*. It is a reinforcing (positive) feedback loop, because there is an even number of – signs in the loop (two of them, in this case). Most of the feedback loop is the same as Figure 9.3. When the *Completion Rate* is low, the *Task Status to Plan* is low (i.e., the task is falling behind schedule), which kicks off more *Corrective Actions*. An increase in *Corrective Actions* leads to an increase in *Number of Resources*. This is the same as in Figure 9.3. However, in the feedback loop in Figure 9.5, an increase in the *Number of Resources* can cause a decrease in the *Resource Productivity*, which causes a decrease in the *"Effective" Resource Hours*, and the cycle starts over again. In his book *The Mythical Man-Month: Essays on Software Engineering* (1975), Frederick P. Brooks, Jr. shows how throwing more people at a late software development project only makes the project later. Unfortunately, this is a common consequence of adding people to a job. The new people require some time to get acquainted with the work. During that time, the experienced people have to spend some of their otherwise productive time teaching the new people about the details of the

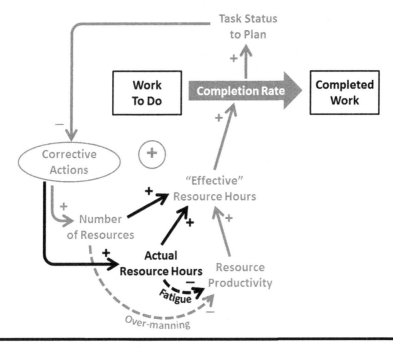

Figure 9.5   Reinforcing feedback loop for over-manning.

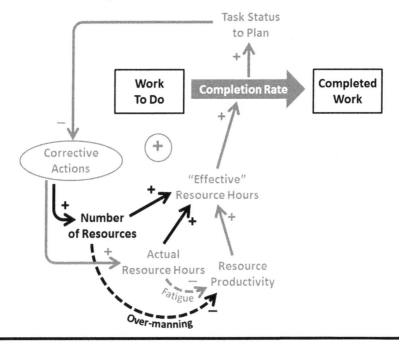

Figure 9.6   Reinforcing feedback loop for fatigue.

work. Also, during that time, the new people will tend to make more mistakes (e.g., defects in production, bugs in software code), which need to be fixed (e.g., rework).

Figure 9.6 shows the reinforcing (positive) feedback loop for *Fatigue*. Most of the feedback loop is the same as in Figure 9.4. When the *Completion Rate* is low, the *Task Status to Plan* is low (i.e., the task is falling behind schedule), which kicks off more *Corrective Actions*. An increase in *Corrective Actions* leads to an increase in *Actual Resource Hours*. This is the same as in Figure 9.4. However, in the feedback loop in Figure 9.6, an increase in the *Actual Resource Hours* can cause a decrease in the *Resource Productivity*, which causes a decrease in the *"Effective" Resource Hours*, and the cycle starts over again. Sometimes, it is possible to work people too hard. They become fatigued and less productive, so the work falls further behind schedule, which puts pressure on management to make the people work even harder, which only slows them down even more, and so on. It becomes a losing battle.

The Simulation Model

Chapter 7 provided an overview of the system dynamics (SD) simulation approach. As stated in Chapter 7, this book is not intended to provide full instructions for developing SD simulations. In this chapter, the reader will see how the consequence map in Figure 9.2 is converted into an SD simulation model and how this model can be used to test several what-if scenarios related to project management. To keep the chapter short and the focus simple, the entire model will not be shown, but the key segments of the model will be described to show how the two feedback loops in Figure 9.4 (crashing with adding overtime) and Figure 9.6 (negative productivity impacts of fatigue) are captured and how these feedback loops interact.

Figure 9.7 shows the task work completion segment of the SD model. There are two stocks: *Work To Do* and *Completed Work* (which match the stocks in Figure 9.2). Notice that the flow between them is *Eff Resource Hours* (equivalent to the *Completion Rate*). Work hours are moved from the backlog of *Work To Do* into the stock *Completed Work* based on the value of *Eff Resource Hours*, which is the product of *Work Hours* (*In Use Labor * Mod Labor Hours*, which is the same as *Number of Resources * Actual Labor Hours* in Figure 9.2) and *Mod Productivity on Labor* (which is the same as *Resource Productivity* in Figure 9.2). There are two other variables at the bottom of Figure 9.7 that are needed for the simulation. *Pct Complete for Task* is the percentage of the total work for the task that has been completed. When this hits 100%, the task is turned "off." *Task Scheduled Start Day* (i.e., the day when the task is scheduled to start) is used to tell the task when to turn "on" compared with *Days* (the current day count in the model). Any variables outside the box in Figure 9.7 are "ghosted" (copied) from other segments of the model.

Figure 9.8 shows the labor hours and labor fatigue segment of the SD model. There is one stock for the level of *Labor Fatigue*, which can range from 0 (no fatigue, fresh) to 100 (completely fatigued, physically unable to do anything).

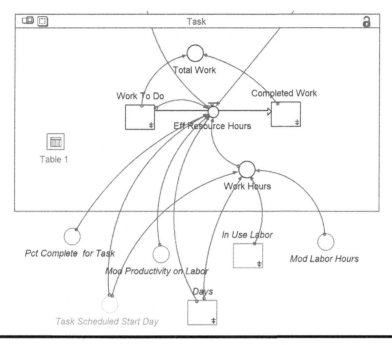

Figure 9.7   Task work completion segment.

Fatigue Generation on the left is the inflow to *Labor Fatigue* and is based on *Overtime Hrs for Labor* (i.e., only the hours above and beyond the normal 8-hour work day) and the *Fatigue per OT Hr* (which is 1 unit of fatigue for every OT hour worked). *Fatigue Dissipation* on the right is the outflow from *Labor Fatigue*. Over a period of time, a person is renewed and no longer fatigued. There is a non-linear relationship with the *Fatigue Dissipation Rate*. When a person is not very fatigued (i.e., *Labor Fatigue* is low), the person recovers fairly quickly (i.e., *Fatigue Dissipation Rate* is high). This is the example of a person working a few overtime hours one day and coming back the next day with no impact. However, when a person is very fatigued (i.e., *Labor Fatigue* is high), the person recovers much more slowly (i.e., *Fatigue Dissipation Rate* is low). This is the example of a person working several weeks of overtime. Even when the person stops working overtime, the next day when the person comes back to work, that person is not completely "fresh." There are lingering effects, and it takes a few days to recover fully. At the top of the box in Figure 9.8, notice that the level of *Labor Fatigue* is an input into the *Fatigue Mult on Productivity*, which is a multiplier that changes the normal productivity level based on the level of fatigue of the workers (the reinforcing feedback loop shown in Figure 9.6). At the bottom of Figure 9.8 outside the box are other variables that essentially calculate any changes in work hours compared with the *Normal Hrs per Labor* and the *Max Allowable Hours* (which is limited to 16, the equivalent of a double shift). This is the balancing feedback loop shown in Figure 9.4. There is a

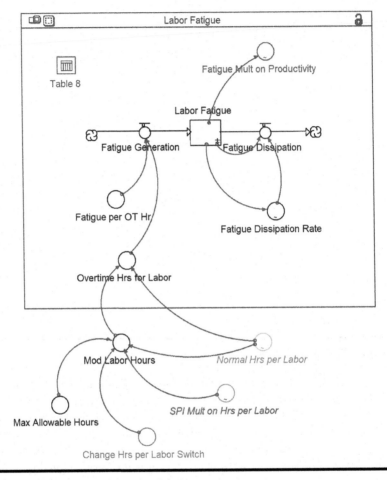

Figure 9.8   Daily labor hours and fatigue segment.

switch that turns on this feedback loop (*Change Hrs per Labor Switch*) and a multiplier based on the schedule performance index (*SPI*) value for the task (*SPI Mult on Hrs per Labor*). By adding switches like this, we can turn on and off different feedback loops to isolate the impacts of each individual feedback loop. If *Change Hrs per Labor Switch* = 1, then the feedback loop will kick in if the conditions in the simulation warrant it. The *SPI Mult on Hrs per Labor* is a multiplier based on the earned value metric *SPI* (to be explained in the next section of this chapter) for the task. The *SPI* essentially provides a status for whether the task is ahead of schedule, on schedule, or behind schedule. If *SPI* = 1.0, the task is exactly on schedule. If *SPI* > 1, the task is ahead of schedule (good). If *SPI* < 1, the task is behind schedule (bad). In this case, if *Change Hrs per Labor Switch* = 1, *Mod Labor Hours* will be adjusted based on the *SPI Mult on Hrs per Labor*, which will change the amount of overtime that employees work and impact the *Labor Fatigue* stock.

Figure 9.9 shows the calculations for the productivity of the employees. The "true" productivity is captured in *Mod Productivity on Labor* and is the product of the *Normal Labor Productivity* (100% or 1.0), *Fatigue Mult on Productivity* (the multiplier on the productivity level based on the level of fatigue, as described in the previous paragraph), and the *Req'd Labor Mult on Productivity* (the multiplier on the productivity level based on the number of employees assigned to the task). Although it is shown in Figure 9.9, *Req'd Labor Mult on Productivity* represents the feedback loop in Figure 9.5 and is not used in this simulation. In the end, *Mod Productivity on Labor* is used in the calculation of *Eff Resource Hours* in Figure 9.7 (i.e., *Completion Rate* from consequence map in Figure 9.2).

In the baseline run for the simulation, all feedback loops are turned off, and the following key parameters are used:

Work To Do = 120 hours
In Use Labor = *Normal Required Labor* = 1 person (not shown in any figures)
Normal Hrs per Labor = *Mod Labor Hours* = 8 hours/day/person
Task Scheduled Start Day = Day 1
Mod Productivity on Labor = 1.0 (100%)

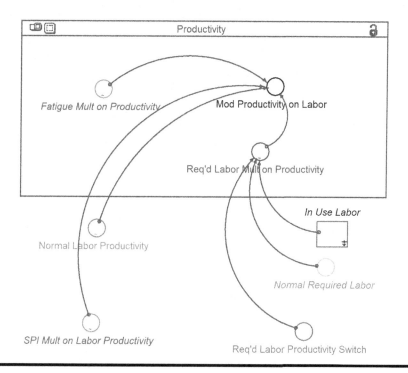

Figure 9.9   Productivity segment.

Given these initial variables, even without running the simulation, we can calculate the expected duration of the task at 15 days, which would put Day 16 as the end date (Day 1 + 15 days = Day 16).

$$\text{Duration} = \text{Work To Do}/$$
$$\left(\text{In Use Labor} \times \text{Mod Labor Hours} \times \text{Mod Productivity on Labor}\right)$$

$$\text{Duration} = 120 \text{ hours}/\left(1 \text{ person} \times 8 \text{ hours/day/person} \times 1.0\right) = 15 \text{ days}$$

Figures 9.10 through 9.12 provide results from the baseline simulation. In these graphs, as well as other graphs in the chapter, the lines on the graph are numbered with the legend provided at the top of the graph. The horizontal axis is time, with a maximum of 20 days for the baseline simulation. On the vertical axis, the stacked numbers (e.g., 1, 2, 3) to the far left match the numbered lines and give the different axis scales for that particular variable. For instance, Figure 9.10 confirms the calculation of the duration at 15 days (start on Day 1 and end on Day 16). (Simulation initialization is Day 0, so nothing happens until Day 1.) This is shown by the variable #1, *Work To Do*, starting at 120 hours on Day 1 and decreasing linearly to 0 hours on Day 16 of the simulation. Notice that variable #2, *Completed Work*, is just the opposite. *Completed Work* begins at 0 hours on Day 1and rises linearly to 120 hours on Day 16. Variable #3, *Cumulative Hours Assigned*, matches *Completed Work*, which indicates that no overtime was worked and no productivity losses were suffered. Every hour that was worked accomplished 1 hour of task work.

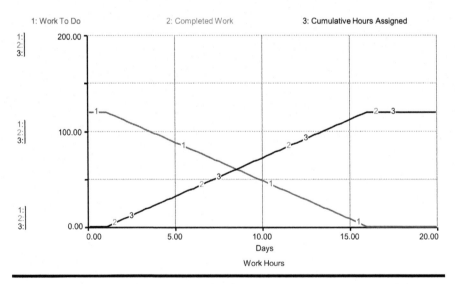

Figure 9.10 Baseline simulation results for work hours.

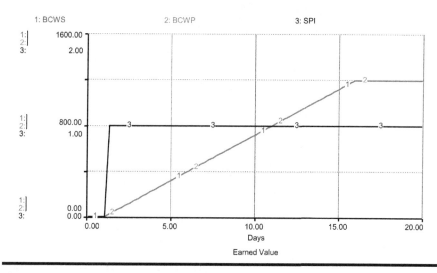

Figure 9.11   Baseline simulation results for earned value.

Figure 9.11 shows some of the key earned value (EV) metrics for this simulation:

BCWS = Budgeted Cost of Work Schedule (this is the proposed schedule for the task)

BCWP = Budgeted Cost of Work Performed (this is the work accomplished for the task)

SPI = Schedule Performance Index (this shows how well the task is on schedule)

As just a quick overview of EV, *BCWS* and *BCWP* are measured in dollars. For this particular task, the hourly pay rate for labor is $10/hour. For a 15-day task with 8 hours worked each day by one person, the end value of *BCWS* = $1200 (15 days * 8 hours/day/person * 1 person * $10/hour). When the task is complete and all the work is finished, *BCWP* = $1200 (the same ending value for *BCWS*).

In Figure 9.11, *BCWS* (variable #1) shows the work accomplishment rate that we want to see on the task. *BCWS* starts at 0 (i.e., $0) and climbs linearly at the rate of 80/day (i.e., $80/day) until it reaches a value of 1200 (i.e., $1200) on Day 16. This represents the steady work rate of one person for 8 hours/day for 15 days. *BCWP* (variable #2) shows the actual work accomplishment. Ideally, we would like to see *BCWP* (variable #2) track exactly with *BCWS* (variable #1), which would indicate that work is getting accomplished exactly as planned. This is the behavior that we see in the baseline simulation results in Figure 9.11: *BCWP* tracks exactly on top of *BCWS*. When *BCWP* = *BCWS* (as desired), then *SPI* = 1, because *SPI* = *BCWP* / *BCWS*. When *SPI* > 1, the task is ahead of schedule (i.e., *BCWP* > *BCWS*, completed work is more than the scheduled work). When *SPI* < 1, the task is behind schedule (i.e., *BCWP* < *BCWS*, completed work is less than the scheduled work). Notice that in Figure 9.10, *SPI* = 1 for all times after the task has started on Day 1.

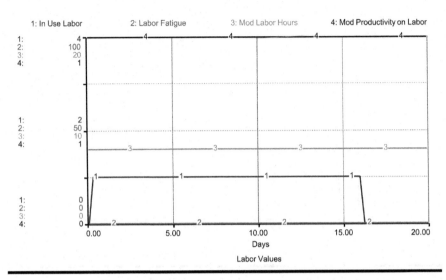

Figure 9.12 Baseline simulation results for labor values.

Figure 9.12 shows additional variables related to the labor for the task. Variable #1 is *In Use Labor*. Notice that this variable starts at 0 at the beginning of the simulation, because the task has not started yet, so no labor is assigned to the task. Then, starting on Day 1, *In Use Labor* increases to 1 (i.e., 1 person) and stays at this level until the task ends on Day 16, at which point *In Use Labor* drops to 0 again (as the person is removed from the completed task). Variable #2 is *Labor Fatigue* and stays at 0 for the entire simulation, because no overtime hours are worked, so there is no accumulation of *Labor Fatigue*. Variable #3 is *Mod Labor Hours*, which remains at 8 for the entire simulation (i.e., the single employee is working 8 hours/day), which confirms that no overtime is worked. If there were overtime, *Mod Labor Hours* would increase above 8 hours/day. Variable #4 is *Mod Productivity on Labor*, which remains at 1 for the entire simulation (i.e., the productivity level for the employees is 100%, so they are fully productive). If overtime is worked, and the employees begin to feel fatigued, *Mod Productivity on Labor* will drop below 1 (i.e., less than 100%).

The following section steps through several scenarios that show the feedback loops begin to kick in and impact task progression. For each scenario, the same three graphs will be shown (as in Figures 9.10 through 9.12) with the same scales for each of the variables on the graphs, so that direct comparison of variables is simplified.

Simulation Scenarios and Results

The first scenario represents a work stoppage for 5 days (Day 4 through Day 9) due to a delay in a material needed for the task. As with the baseline, the feedback loops

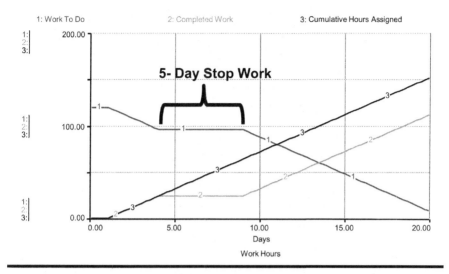

Figure 9.13   Scenario 1 simulation results for work hours.

are still turned off. As expected, work stops for 5 days, as shown in Figure 9.13: *Work To Do* (variable #1) and *Completed Work* (variable #2) remain steady for the 5 days during the work stoppage. Notice that *Cumulative Hours Assigned* (variable #3) continues to accumulate, because the employee working on the task is still assigned to the task and must be paid.

Figure 9.14 shows the impact of the material delay (work stoppage) on the EV metrics. Because the due date for the task has not changed and remains Day 16,

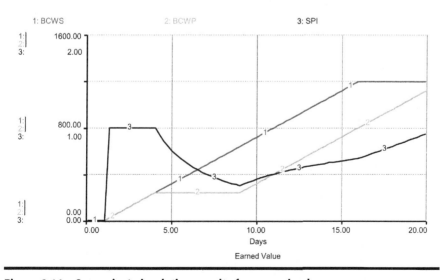

Figure 9.14   Scenario 1 simulation results for earned value.

BCWS (variable #1) looks the same as it does in the baseline in Figure 9.11 with a linear increase of 8 hours each day from Day 1 (*BCWS* = 0) to Day 16 (*BCWS* = 1200). However, notice that *BCWP* (variable #2), which represents work performed, stays flat for Day 4 through Day 9 of the work stoppage. Because *BCWS* continues to increase for these 5 days while *BCWP* stays the same, *SPI* falls below 1, since *SPI* = *BCWP* / *BCWS*. *SPI* never gets back to the value of 1 for the remainder of the simulation, because the task is behind schedule for the rest of the simulation. Notice that the task still has not finished by Day 20 (the last day of the simulation), as shown by the line for variable #2, because it never quite reaches 1200 (representing all work completed).

Figure 9.15 shows the results for this scenario for the labor values. Because no feedback loops are turned on, the values on this graph look exactly the same as in the baseline scenario. Only one person is working on the task with no overtime, so there is no fatigue and therefore, no productivity losses.

Scenario 2 is the same as Scenario 1 with the 5-day work stoppage, but the feedback loops in Figure 9.4 and Figure 9.6 are now turned on, so that hours will be adjusted for the labor based on how well the task is performing to schedule, and productivity consequences associated with fatigue will be included. Essentially, this feedback loop from Figure 9.4 allows overtime hours to be added when the task falls behind schedule. Then, as overtime is applied, fatigue kicks in and productivity is impacted (feedback loop in Figure 9.6). Figure 9.16 shows the "multiplier" table function that relates the value of *SPI* (the EV metric that indicates how well the task is doing compared with its planned schedule) with a multiplier on the normal labor hours (i.e., 8 hours/day/person). For example, when the multiplier is 2, then we have the following "doubling" of daily work hours:

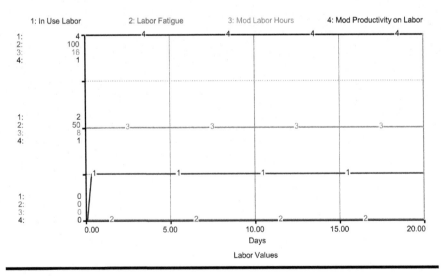

Figure 9.15 Scenario 1 simulation results for labor values.

Mod Hours per Labor = SPI Mult on Hrs per Labor × Normal Labor Hours

Mod Hours per Labor = 2.0 × 8 hours/day/person = 16 hours/day/person

Note: In Scenario 2, *only* the labor hours feedback loop is turned on. The other feedback loops in Figure 9.3 and Figure 9.5 related to the number of resources assigned to the task are still turned off and will not be used in any of the scenarios.

In the table shown on the right side of Figure 9.16, the left column is the *SPI* value, and the right column is the multiplier value (*SPI Mult on Hrs per Labor*). If *SPI* = 1, the task is right on schedule, so the multiplier value is 1.0 (so that employees work the regular 8 hours/day). However, when *SPI* < 1, it indicates that the task is falling behind schedule. The lower the *SPI* value, the further the task is behind schedule (e.g., *SPI* = 0.50 means that the task is further behind schedule than if *SPI* = 0.75). In the table in Figure 9.16, when *SPI* drops to 0.90, the multiplier is 2 (which indicates doubling hours from 8 hours/day to 16 hours/day). When *SPI* is lower than 0.90, the multiplier goes up to 2.5 (indicating a 20-hour work day). In this particular example, remember that the *Max Allowable Hours* is set at 16. Even if the multiplier became 2.5 to push for a 20-hour work day, the employees would still be limited to 16 hours/day.

For Scenario 2, Figure 9.17 shows the results for work hours, Figure 9.18 shows the results for earned value, and Figure 9.19 shows the results for labor values. In Figure 9.18 (earned value), because of the 5-day delay, *BCWP* falls below *BCWS*,

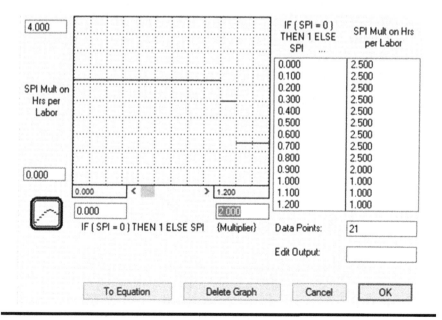

Figure 9.16 Multiplier on normal labor hours based on SPI value.

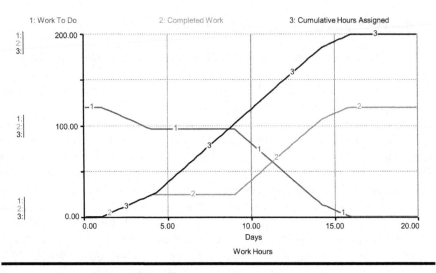

Figure 9.17   Scenario 2 simulation results for work hours.

so *SPI* < 1 (similarly to what is seen in Figure 9.14 for Scenario 1). However, since the labor hours feedback loop is turned on, this decrease in *SPI* kicks off additional labor hours. Figure 9.19 shows that *Mod Labor Hours* jumps from 8 to 16 (due to the multiplier of 2). Now, the single employee is working 8 hours of overtime per day (double shift). Consequently, *Labor Fatigue* increases from 0 to a maximum of about 32 (e.g., 32% fatigued) on Day 14, and a slight drop in productivity (*Mod Productivity on Labor*) occurs because of this fatigue. Fortunately, the drop is not too bad, because this fatigue is not prolonged at a high level. The overtime only

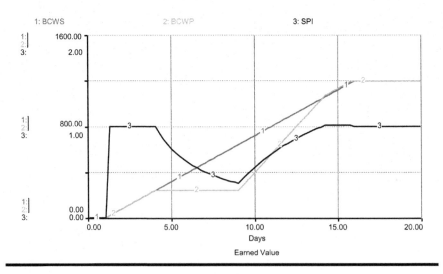

Figure 9.18   Scenario 2 simulation results for earned value.

lasts about 2 weeks, so recovery is fairly quick. *Mod Productivity on Labor* drops to a minimum of about 0.96 on Day 14. The increase in work hours gets the task back on schedule, because the productivity drop is not too severe (*Completed Work* reaches 1200 on Day 16 in Figure 9.17, and *SPI* gets back to 1 on Day 16 in Figure 9.18). If the task were more than 120 hours long, the productivity impact would be greater, because overtime would have to be endured for a longer period of time. In this example scenario, the productivity impact due to fatigue is minimal. But, it is easy to see that a situation could be experienced in which an employee working on multiple tasks could experience enough overtime to cause his or her productivity to drop to a "tipping point," after which he or she becomes less and less productive as management assigns more and more overtime hours. This will be explored in Scenario 3.

Notice in Scenario 2 that *In Use Labor* in Figure 9.19 remains at 1 (i.e., one employee), because the feedback loop for the number of resources is not turned on. That is, the feedback loop shown in Figure 9.4 is turned on in Scenario 2, but the feedback loop in Figure 9.3 is still turned off. As a result, we see that management tries to keep the task on schedule by *only* changing the hours that people work, *not* by adding labor.

Scenario 3 is similar to Scenario 2 with the labor hours and fatigue feedback loops turned on. However, in Scenario 3, the work stoppage is extended to make the task fall further behind to push the feedback loops to the tipping point where the fatigue feedback loop overpowers the crashing feedback loop. Figures 9.20 through 9.22 provide the simulation results for Scenario 3. In the figures for Scenario 3, the simulation duration is extended to 60 days to allow ample time for all the feedback loops to play out. For this same reason, the *Work To Do* is increased to 240 hours.

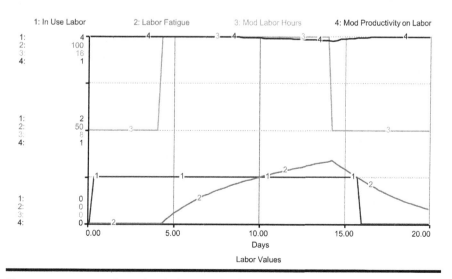

Figure 9.19   Scenario 2 simulation results for labor values.

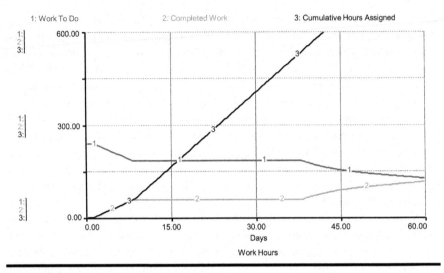

Figure 9.20   Scenario 3 simulation results for work hours.

In addition, the vertical scales have been changed on Figures 9.20 and 9.21 to accommodate the increase in work.

Figure 9.20 shows the extended work stoppage to force a delay in the task completion (notice the flat line in *Work To Do* and *Completed Work* in the middle of the simulation). As seen in Figure 9.20, *Work To Do* never reaches zero, so the task never finishes. In fact, by the end of the simulation, it appears that *Work To Do* (and *Completed Work*) begins to level out. Because the extended work stoppage

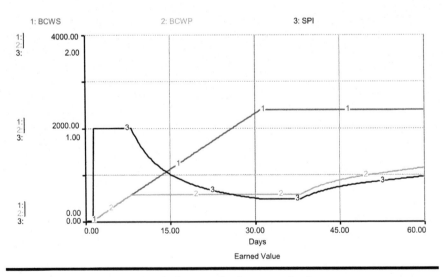

Figure 9.21   Scenario 3 simulation results for earned value.

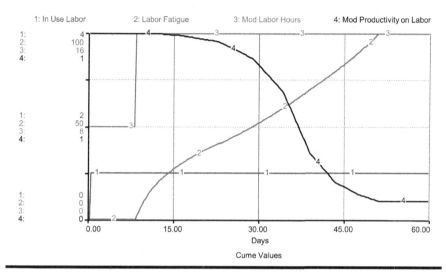

Figure 9.22   Scenario 3 simulation results for labor values.

causes the task to fall so far behind (as indicated in Figure 9.21 by the drop in *SPI* well below 1), overtime hours are added for an extended period of time, as shown by the rise in *Mod Labor Hours*. Notice that once *Mod Labor Hours* rises to 16 with overtime, it stays at that level for the rest of the simulation, because productivity (*Mod Productivity on Labor*) drops significantly due to high *Labor Fatigue*. In this scenario, the long amount of overtime does not allow the employee to recover. Instead, the employee reaches such a low level of productivity that the employee is not getting any further with the work accomplishment for the task (as shown by the leveling of *Work To Do* and *Completed Work* in Figure 9.20).

Final Remarks

As stated several times in this chapter, the reader should be aware that this is not the full simulation for the task. The book *The Dynamic Progress Method: Using Advanced Simulation to Improve Project Planning and Management* (White, Sholtes, 2016), discusses more elements, as Figure 9.1 portrays. For example, cost is never considered in these scenarios. Working overtime and adding resources cost more money, so there are additional feedback loops related to how management corrects the cost of the task (e.g., by reducing hours or reducing labor). The scenarios in this chapter focused on only one management corrective action (crashing with overtime) and the feedback loop associated with the corresponding productivity losses due to fatigue from working overtime. The purpose is to show the reader how simulation helps to quantify the behaviors explored in a consequence map. In particular, when it comes to managing projects, simply "knowing" that there are feedback loops that might impact performance is not enough. Project managers need to know specific details to ensure that the right amount of labor is used, the right number of hours are worked, and the cost and schedule objectives for the project are met. Thus, project managers need to move beyond consequence maps and into simulation to address these types of specific details.

Bibliography

Brooks, Jr., Frederick P., *The Mythical Man-Month: Essays on Software Engineering*, Reading, MA: Addison-Wesley, 1975.

White, J. Chris and Sholtes, Robert M., *The Dynamic Progress Method: Using Advanced Simulation to Improve Project Planning and Management*, Boca Raton, FL: CRC Press, 2016.

STRUCTURED FOR SUCCESS

4

Chapter 10

Structured for Success

"I should estimate that in my experience most troubles and most possibilities for improvement add up to the proportions something like this: 94% belongs to the system (responsibility of management), 6% special."

Dr. W. Edwards Deming, *Out of the Crisis*, **MIT Press, p. 248**

Individual Control and System Control

For me, the work of this book started in 1987, when I read the passage by Dr. W. Edwards Deming in his book *Out of the Crisis* (1982) quoted at the beginning of this chapter. At the time, the main point that I took from this passage was that 94% of problems are caused by the management of a company. As a young engineer in my first job, I was on the side of the front-line employees, so I enjoyed seeing a passage like this. However, over the years, I came to realize the full magnitude of this passage. The systems that are in place at organizations are the source of many problems within organizations, and management puts those systems in place. Thus, management (by putting ineffective systems in place and/or allowing those systems to stay in place) causes 94% of the problems. One could argue that the true number may not be 94%. But, I definitely believe that it is extremely high.

In fact, it led me to draw the following graphic on the back of an envelope, literally, at dinner one night. In Figure 10.1, there are two aspects considered: control by the individual (Individual Control) and control by the system (System Control). By now, the reader should be familiar with the use of the word *system* to encompass a wide range of things, from organizations to issues. In organizational systems, there is a peculiar relationship between the individual parts of the system (employees) and the relations among those parts. Most organizations have a personnel structure

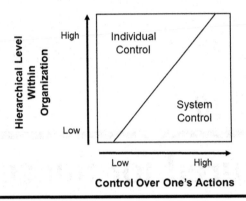

Figure 10.1 Individual control vs. system control.

that is hierarchical. Due to the nature of a hierarchy, the employees at one level of the hierarchy are influenced by decisions and actions taken at the next higher level in the hierarchy. In some cases, the influences are very strong, such as the enforcement of a company directive or procedure. In this case, the influence can be considered a control. Such controls limit the authority of an individual employee over his or her own job activities. As a result, the lowest levels of the hierarchy in an organization tend to be dominated by external controls and influences simply because of their location in the hierarchy.

In an organizational hierarchy, people, as individual parts of the system, are used to actually represent system groups within the organization. For example, a manager might have many employees doing work in her unit, but on the organizational chart, the manager's name is used to represent that unit. With the position typically comes the authority to make decisions concerning that specific unit. The higher the position in the hierarchy, the larger the portion of the total system that is represented. This, of course, is one of the main purposes of a hierarchy. The theory is that if there is a problem between two different work groups, there has to be someone above both of the work groups to oversee and administer a solution. At the very top of the organization, the president or CEO represents the entire organizational system and typically has the authority to make decisions concerning the entire organization. Thus, an individual part of the system (i.e., the employee who is the CEO) has significant control over the entire system (i.e., the directives and procedures that the other employees must use).

In Figure 10.1, Individual Control is the level of control an individual has over his or her own job activities, actions, and decisions within a system. Conversely, System Control is the level of control exerted by the system to sway or mandate an individual's job activities, actions, and decisions (via policies, directives, processes, procedures, etc.). In Figure 10.1, the horizontal axis shows the share of control going to Individual Control and System Control. The vertical axis represents the job or responsibility level of a person within the system (e.g., organization).

As extreme examples, consider a CEO of an organization and a junior-level employee at the same organization. The CEO at the top of the organizational hierarchy has a high degree of individual control within their defined role, which can also be used to create the organization's *systems* of operation. On the other hand, the junior-level employee has very little individual control and, instead, is primarily controlled by the *systems* put in place by others higher in the organizational hierarchy (e.g., directors, vice presidents, C-level). This is shown by the slanted line going from the lower left of the graphic to the upper right of the graphic.

At low levels of the organization (in terms of job or authority hierarchy), there is some Individual Control, but it is far outweighed by System Control. In other words, employees at the lower levels of the organizational hierarchy do have some control, but most of their activities are dictated by processes, policies, or directives established for the organization. Consider an assembly line worker who must paint a box white. The color white has been decided by someone else, as well as the type of brush that will be used, but the assembly line worker still has the choice to do his or her best. In this example, the color of the paint, the box to be painted, and the paint brush are all controlled by other employees higher in the organizational hierarchy. Thus, the assembly line worker must live with these decisions. This represents System Control over job activities. Yet, it should be noted that no matter how low an employee is in the hierarchy, that employee still has some individual control over his or her job activities (i.e., whether or not to do his or her best).

At high levels of the organizational hierarchy, this has shifted, so that there is a much larger amount of Individual Control and a smaller amount of System Control. For instance, if a high-level employee desires to take a day off to go play golf, that individual usually has the power and authority to do so somewhat freely and without consequences. However, the CEO does not have complete freedom. He or she still has certain financial processes to follow and a board of directors to whom he or she reports.

This directly supports Deming's comment about management (and leaders). In Chapter 1, I stated that a leader can be anyone who produces change in the system, regardless of where they are in the system. For this discussion, we are going to take the view of a leader as the top-level management of an organization. Leaders, because of their location in the organizational hierarchy, have the opportunity to put in place the systems (i.e., structures) that will guide the behavior of others lower down in the organizational hierarchy. The old interpretation of this dynamic would be that *power corrupts, and absolute power corrupts absolutely.* Once in the hierarchical position of power (i.e., at the top of the hierarchy), that person can put in place systems and structures that benefit the person and make it more difficult for others to usurp power. However, this book is trying to give it a new interpretation: that *leaders can positively influence cultures and change.*

Which leads us to the current leadership problem: Today's leadership issues are a result of personal actions of leaders and the organizational structures put in place by these leaders. There is a plethora of examples of high-level company or government officials acting unethically, implementing policies, or taking actions that benefit them personally but not the organization or system as a whole. How does this happen? As shown in Figure 10.1, leaders typically control the organizational system at high levels with little organizational control of their actions. Over time and without support or accountability, a leader's "gray" areas tend to grow. Situations that might be black-and-white to most of us, with very clear "right and wrong" answers, tend to get rationalized and defended by the leader who stands to gain from the situation. And so, we have our dilemma, which creates the problem: The leader who has the ability to put the proper system structures in place is often not motivated to do so. Unfortunately, many leaders (who may have the interests of others in mind) do not realize that they have this type of power and influence, so they do not put the proper system structures in place. Or, these leaders do not understand the power of the organizational system structure for driving the behaviors of others in the organization, and so they feel that the only way to enforce change is to be authoritative, demanding, and punitive. This is the old type of leadership, which must be replaced by the leader who is a master of structure.

Structure Follows Strategy

I used the term *proper system structures* in the previous paragraph to imply that proper structures are the structures that will help the organization succeed. In Chapter 1, I used the phrase *structured for success* to indicate the ability of leaders to put system structures in place that will guide employee behavior toward what has been defined as "success" for the organization. (*Disclaimer*: This book is not about defining that "success." There are plenty of books out there that help define what success should look like. Instead, this book focuses on the influence of structures to impact that success.)

Figure 10.2 captures this notion, and it extends from Figure 1.5 in Chapter 1. Structure guides behavior, so the system structure is the area for greatest leverage and probability of success when trying to implement a strategy or change. To be fully effective, an organization's strategy must be manifested and supported by system structures that guide behavior toward the goals and objectives of that strategy. To put it another way, if the structure of the organization *does not* support the organization's overall strategy and direction, the strategy will have a significantly *lower probability* of success, or perhaps even be doomed to failure from the start.

As stated in Chapter 1, leadership is about change. Leadership is about moving a group of people in a certain direction to accomplish a certain objective or set of objectives. Leadership does not exist if there is nothing to accomplish. "Moving a group of people" implies guiding or controlling their behaviors. Behavior control sounds a bit antagonistic, but it is essential, nonetheless, to effective leadership. Thus, effective leaders must know how to guide and influence people's behavior. Much previous research has judged the efficacy of leaders by their ability to

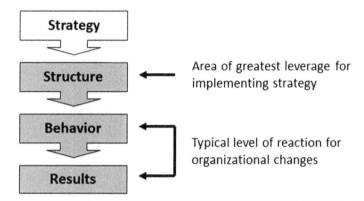

Figure 10.2 Successful strategies for change are supported by appropriate structures.

persuade and motivate others. However, this is only a small part of what is needed to influence others in the organization. System structures are the key.

Integrated Model of Change

Systems theorists, such as Jay Forrester, Robert Fritz, and Peter Senge, contend that structure in social systems guides behavior similarly to mechanical and electrical feedback systems. The way different individual parts of the system are combined together and interrelated strongly influences their individual performance as well as the overall system performance. For example, in an organization, the financial accounting system is a type of structure that influences the behavior or actions of employees. Since leadership is all about guiding behavior, and system structure guides behavior, it is important to grasp fully the operational mechanics of Figure 10.3, which is an integrated model of change rooted in system structure. In this figure, it should be noted that system structures can be *external* to an individual, such as processes and directives, as previously discussed in this book. Yet, system structures can also be *internal* to an individual, such as belief systems, motivation, confidence, and so on, which also guide individual behaviors and actions (e.g., as seen in the consequence map in Chapter 7 with employee motivation/ enthusiasm, etc.).

In Figure 10.3, the reader will notice that there are arrows that go from the top of the figure down to the bottom as well as arrows that go from the bottom of the figure to the top. All of these arrows relate individual beliefs and behaviors to group beliefs and behaviors. The arrows moving from bottom to top show that change can start with the seed of a single individual's beliefs or attitudes. Imagine a civic leader with a new view of government or an entrepreneur with a new business idea. It starts with the individual holding a strong belief or attitude (which is *internal*

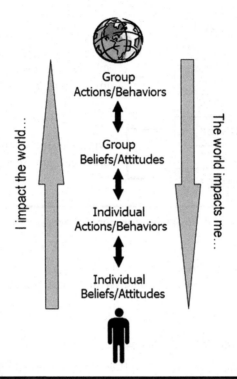

Figure 10.3   Bottom-up and top-down integrated model of change.

to the individual), so strong that it alters the outward behavior of the individual. Based on the new belief, the individual acts and behaves in a new way. Eventually, other people who are friends with the individual, work with the individual, or are exposed to the individual through other settings (i.e., society, church, clubs) begin to change their beliefs and attitudes because of the strong conviction and example of the single individual. Now, there is a larger group (which is *external* to the individual) that has a change in beliefs or attitudes, which are eventually manifested in the group's actions and behaviors. This represents bottom-up change that goes from an individual to a larger group.

In Figure 10.3, the arrows moving from top to bottom show the opposite. Group behaviors (which are *external* to the individual) can be controlled (through laws, directives, etc.) to exhibit a new behavior. The change in group behavior can influence the beliefs and attitudes of the group as a whole, which can impact the actions and behaviors of the various individuals and finally impact the beliefs and attitudes of the various individuals (which are *internal* to the individual). Here is a personal example. When I was a teenager in the 1980s, a new law was introduced: mandatory seat belts for drivers. It is difficult even to think back prior to that time, when I would never wear a seat belt in the car. But, I never did. There was no requirement for me to do so. It was optional. At first, I (and many others) didn't like the law. Wearing a seat belt was uncomfortable, and it would wrinkle my shirt. However, I was a law-abiding citizen, so I complied. Over time, I changed my attitude toward seat belts. They are extremely important, and they save lives. I cannot imagine riding in a car today without wearing a seat belt. In fact, if the law changed and seat belts were no longer required, I would still wear one. In this example, a permanent change took place. An external group behavior resulted in a change in an individual's internal beliefs.

However, not all top-down changes are as successful. Consider taxes added to cigarettes. Although it is not the primary purpose of the tax, one of the purposes of the tax is to discourage smoking, because it has been deemed unhealthy. And to some extent, the taxes do discourage and reduce smoking. Due to the high cost of cigarettes, people curtail their smoking, because they simply cannot afford it. From this vantage point, the tax looks like an effective policy to reduce smoking. Yet, if the tax were removed, many people who reduced their smoking would most likely immediately increase their smoking, because the financial barrier had been removed. In this example, the external top-down attempt at change cannot be considered successful. No change is permanent unless it makes it to the level of the internal beliefs and attitudes of the individual. Let me repeat that. Until an individual holds a firm belief about something, that individual will not fundamentally change his or her behavior. That individual may be "controlled" in some ways by threats of punishment, embarrassment, exclusion, or the like, but as soon as those controls are removed, the individual will revert to previous behaviors. Only when the individual truly changes his or her beliefs, assumptions, or attitudes toward something will that individual truly change his or her behavior. In the case of the smoking example, an internal control (or structure) is to teach people about the unhealthy and undesirable consequences of smoking, so that they decide, regardless of the price of cigarettes, that they do not want to smoke.

There are several characteristics associated with bottom-up, internally driven behavior change and control. These are summarized in Figure 10.4. Bottom-up change takes a long time before results are seen at the group behavior level. It takes a period of time before an individual change in belief is manifested in an individual's actions, and then it takes more time before the group adopts this same belief and it is manifested in the group's actions. However, this type of change is more permanent, because all those involved truly believe and embrace the change in belief that drives their actions. The bottom-up approach is sometimes called a *participative* approach, because the behavior change or control for the whole group begins with the individuals in the group. Consequently, the individuals are proactively choosing their destiny and making their own decisions.

There are several characteristics associated with top-down, externally driven behavior change and control. Top-down change only takes a short period of time before results are seen at the group behavior level, because this is where the change or control is being applied (i.e., processes, directives). However, it takes a longer

> ## Structure guides behavior.

Characteristics of "external" structures:
• Top-down direction with focus on group behaviors
• <u>Examples</u>: Laws, policies, processes
• Control culture that works because of fear
• Behavior often stops when control is removed

Characteristics of "internal" structures:
• Bottom-up direction with focus on individual principles
• <u>Examples</u>: Entrepreneurs, strong "spirited" individuals
• Empowerment culture that works because of choice
• Behavior is more permanent

Figure 10.4   Characteristics of internal and external structures.

period of time before the beliefs and attitudes of the individuals change due to the group behavior change. This type of behavior change is often less permanent, because it is being "forced" on the individuals through processes, policies, and other structures. Typically, group behavior will regress to the previous behavior when the control is removed. This is because the individuals are not freely choosing their destiny. Instead, they are being governed by external processes and are usually fearful of the consequences if they do not comply.

In this book, the definition of leadership is the ability to influence other individuals' beliefs and behaviors in such a way that the individuals accept the new beliefs and behaviors associated with the desired change. As a result, the effective leader has a two-pronged duty. As well as serving as an example and role model for the change (i.e., internal perspective), the effective leader also makes the right decisions and implements the right processes, policies, and directives that support the change (i.e., external perspective). Sounds simple. However, in many cases, the internal beliefs and attitudes espoused by the change do not match the external processes and controls within which the individuals must work. The external processes and controls must drive the same behavior that the beliefs and attitudes drive. Otherwise, there is a major disconnect, and the individual has to make the choice whether to follow the espoused beliefs of the change or to follow the institutionalized processes and controls that do not support the change. In this case, when there is disharmony between the internal beliefs of the change and the implemented external controls, the individual must constantly battle against the "system" to continue to act in accordance with the desired beliefs. This combat requires a great deal of energy and effort. Eventually, most individuals will wear down and simply succumb to the external controls, which means that the change was never internalized and therefore, will not become permanent.

In Robert Fritz's words (Fritz, 1984), this is the "path of least resistance." The path of least resistance is the pathway carved by the system structure, like water running through a riverbed carved in the side of a mountain. The riverbed guides the water. When there are two conflicting system structures (one external and one internal), there is no path of least resistance. There are now two paths, and the individual must make a choice which structure to follow (i.e., which structure to allow to guide the individual's behavior).

An easy example of this type of disharmony is a situation in which an organization tries to move to a team-oriented environment while keeping the same old function-oriented controls and incentives in place. The message from upper management is that we are all on the same team and we all float or sink together. There is no "I" in "team," etc. Most people would agree with this message and would enjoy working in such a team-oriented environment. However, the organization typically still has that same function-oriented performance appraisal process in place. Now, an electrical engineer on a "team" has to decide whether he or she will do something that helps the team or do something that helps himself or herself. The electrical engineer is evaluated (and receives pay increases and bonuses) by his or her functional supervisor (i.e., engineering manager) based on how well he or she does electrical engineering. That individual is not evaluated based on how well the team does. The message of being a team is in direct conflict with the function-oriented controls that are in place. Why help the team when there is no payoff? At first, the electrical engineer may try hard to keep a team-oriented attitude and do things that support the team without highlighting the individual's own contributions. But after the next performance appraisal, when the electrical engineer sees his or her fellow engineers get raises because they did things to help themselves and not their teams, that electrical engineer will shift back to a function-orientation to try to meet the financial incentives for the next evaluation period. This is a terrible situation in which to put the employee. The message that wants everyone to hold the *internal* belief that they are a team with a shared destiny is not supported by the *external* processes associated with the performance evaluations. In 90% of these types of disconnects, the individual will usually give in to the external processes that do not support the desired change (because the consequences of not following the external structures are typically much greater than the consequences of not following the internal structures). As a result, the change ultimately fails, because the two system structures are not aligned and do not drive the same behavior.

Within an organization, if anyone ever has to "fight the system" or "go around the system" to get something accomplished in the organization, this is a big red flag that the processes and policies of the organization do not naturally generate the desired behavior or course of action (i.e., there is a disconnect between external and internal structures). The effective leader ensures that these types of battle do not occur. Make the system such that the "right behavior" or "right decisions" occur naturally and without any philosophical struggle.

Effective Leaders Are Masters of Structure

The effective leader, as a master of structure, understands that both internal and external structures are needed for permanent change and that these internal and external structures must consistently drive the exact same behavior. As a result, leaders are needed who can simultaneously act as personal examples of the desired change (to drive the bottom-up part of the integrated model of change in Figure 10.3) while architecting the right systems for the organization (to drive the top-down part of the integrated model of change in Figure 10.3). The effective leader knows that organizational transformation and change first requires individual transformation and change. Lead by example.

However, while internal structures tend to make the changes permanent in the long run, often the external structures are needed in the near term to act as a forcing function toward the new behavior. These external structures and controls need to stay in place long enough for the internal structures to kick in to make the change permanent. In many cases, it is often best simply to maintain the external structures and controls indefinitely to ensure that the new behavior is truly permanent. With both external and internal structures in place, the probability for successful change is highest. In this situation, no matter which structure the employee may be more influenced by, the final resulting behavior or change is the same: the desired behavior or change.

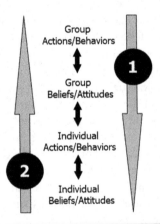

Any new behavior requires external controls until internal controls develop, and even then there may still be a need for external controls.

Figure 10.5 Internal structures drive permanent change, but external structures are often needed to drive the initial change.

As a quick summary, issues arise in organizations when internal and external structures and controls contradict each other. These contradicting structures make it difficult for the employee to "do the right thing," because what it means to "do the right thing" is not clear. The worst situation to put an employee in is one in which the best action is not clear. Effective leaders (i.e., those leaders who are masters of structure) work to align the internal and external structures so that both sets of structures drive the exact same behavior. In this situation, whether the employee is more driven by external controls (i.e., psychologically speaking, the employee has an external locus of control) or more driven by internal controls (i.e., the employee has an internal locus of control), the behavior exhibited by that employee is the desired behavior that will lead to the desired performance results.

Bibliography

Chandler, Alfred D., Jr., *Strategy and Structure: Chapters in the History of the American Industrial Enterprise*, Cambridge, MA: The MIT Press, 1962.

Deming, W. Edwards, *Out of the Crisis*, Cambridge, MA: The MIT Press, 1982.

Fritz, Robert, *The Path of Least Resistance*, Salem, MA: Stillpoint, 1984.

Pryor, Mildred G., White, J. Chris, and Toombs, Leslie, *Strategic Quality Management: A Strategic Systems Approach to Continuous Improvement*, Boston, MA: Cengage Learning, 2007.

White, J. Chris, Pinder, Margaret, and Honker, Linda, Final Report for Phase I SBIR Project, U.S. Army Small Business Innovative Research (SBIR) Program, Delivered to Dr. Jon Fallesen, 2002.

Index

Asset management, for city water delivery
system, 51–59

BAC, *see* Branding and Collaboration Group
(BAC)
Balancing feedback loop, *see* Negative feedback
loop
Bathtub analogy, 120–121
Beer Game, 119–120
Behavior, pattern of, 8–10
Bottom-up approach, 181
Branding and Collaboration Group (BAC), 127
Brooks, Frederick P., 156

Cash balance model, 121–124
Cause-and-effect relationship, 44–45,
47–48, 50
Center for Scientific Research (CSR), 28
Change initiative, and consequence map, 61–78
feedback loop, 61–74
management, 75–76
overview, 61
Change in state, 18–19, 23–24
Coefficient of determination, 118
Complex systems, 12
Consequence map, 28
and city for change initiative, 61–78
feedback loop, 61–74
management, 75–76
overview, 61
creating, 43–59
asset management for city water delivery
system, 51–59
cause-and-effect connections, 44–45,
47–48, 50
closing loops, 50–51
identifying feedback loops, 48–49
iterations and, 51

laundry lists and circles, 46–47
nouns and relationships, 44–46
overview, 43
team-based development, 43
and management culture for defense
contractor, 91–107
feedback loops, 98–102
issues and intervention, 102–106
overview, 91–92
program performance, 93–98
for non-profit organization, 79–89
feedback loop, 82–86
intervention, 86–88
overview, 79
for proposal process, 81–82
reinforcing loop for rework and capacity
constraints, 80–81
and project management, 151–154
and reduction in force (RIF), 127–131
"Conveyance Catch-22," 52
Crashing, 151, 152
CSR, *see* Center for Scientific Research (CSR)

Data Integrity, 99–102
Deming, W. Edwards, 175
*The Dynamic Progress Method: Using Advanced
Simulation to Improve Project
Planning and Management,* 151

Executive bump, 88
Executive management, 86–88

Feedback loops, 10–11, 37–39
closing, 50–51
in consequence map, 61–74, 82–86
for change initiative, 61–71
for management culture, 98–102
for non-profit organization, 82–86

identifying, 48–49
loose, 38
multiple, 28–35
negative, 20–23, 48
overview, 15–16
positive, 16–19, 48
project management, 154–158
reduction in force (RIF), 131–134
and S-curve, 23–27
tight, 38
Forrester, Jay, 12, 119
Fritz, Robert, 183

Individual control *vs.* system control, 175–178
Industrial Dynamics, 120
Integrated product team (IPT), 92, 94

Kaibab Plateau, 35–37

Leaders and structures, ix–x, 3–13, 177
Leadership, ix, 3, 177, 178
Lean Six Sigma project, 59, 73–76
Learning feedback loop, 8
Leverage, ix, 12
Linear trend, 118–119
Loose feedback loop, 38

Maintenance death spiral, 52–53
Management culture, and consequence map,
        91–107
    feedback loops, 98–102
    issues and intervention, 102–106
    overview, 91–92
    program performance, 93–98
Management by walking around (MBWA), 86
Massachusetts Institute of Technology
        (MIT), 35, 119
MBWA, *see* Management by walking around
        (MBWA)
MIT, *see* Massachusetts Institute of Technology
        (MIT)
MIT Sloan School of Management, 36
Multiple feedback loops, 28–35
*The Mythical Man-Month: Essays on Software
        Engineering,* 156

National Institutes of Health (NIH), 28–35
Negative feedback loop, 20–23
    for citizen satisfaction, 61–63
    for training decrease, 69–70
NIH, *see* National Institutes of Health (NIH)

Non-profit organization, consequence map for,
        79–89
    feedback loop, 82–86
    intervention, 86–88
    overview, 79
    for proposal process, 81–82
    reinforcing loop for rework and capacity
            constraints, 80–81
Nouns and relationships, 44–46

Out of the Crisis, 175

Participative approach, *see* Bottom-up approach
Path of least resistance, 183
Polynomial trend, 118–119
Positive feedback loop, 16–19
    for employee fatigue, 70–71
    for employee motivation, 63–64
    for employee productivity, 64–65
    for employee turnover, 71
    and improvements, 66–68
    for management support and motivation,
            65–66
    and productivity, 68–69
Project management, 151–172
    and consequence map, 151–154
    feedback loops, 154–158
    overview, 151
    scenarios and results, 164–174
    SD simulation model, 158–164

Reduction in force (RIF), 127–150
    and consequence map, 127–131
    feedback loops, 131–134
    scenarios and results, 141–149
    SD model, 134–141
Reinforcing feedback loop, *see* Positive feedback
        loop
RIF, *see* Reduction in force (RIF)

S-curve, 23–27
SD, *see* System dynamics (SD)
State of system, 18–19, 22–23, 24, 32
Sterman, John, 35
Structure and success, ix, 175–185
    effective leader, x, 184–185
    individual control *vs.* system control,
            175–178
    integrated model of change, 179–183
    strategy, 178–179
System Dynamics Group, 35

System dynamics (SD), 111–125
    models and simulation, 119–124
    overview, 111
    project management, 58–164
    reduction in force (RIF), 134–141
    statistical modeling, 112–119
    structural modeling, 112–119

Team-based development, 43
Tight feedback loop, 38
Top-down approach, 181

Vicious/virtuous cycle, 16

Water Efficiency (magazine), 52

Printed in the United States
by Baker & Taylor Publisher Services